monsoonbooks

JAKARTA UNDERCOVER II

Moammar Emka was born in the village of Jetak-Montong in East Java, Indonesia. While completing his education at the Government Institute for Islamic Studies in Jakarta, he wrote for several regional and national newspapers on social, political and religious issues.

From the mid-nineties, Moammar Emka worked for a variety of newspapers and magazines, never straying far from the world of entertainment journalism. At *Berita Yudha*, *Prospek* and *Popular*, his columns were widely read for their insights into Jakarta's popular culture and high-society life.

In addition to being a consultant and contributor at *X Men's Magazine*, a host on SCTV's MALEM 2, a freelance writer and a photographer, Moammar Emka also runs his own business in the entertainment and public relations sector.

He is the bestselling author of *Jakarta Undercover*, *Jakarta Undercover II* and *Jakarta Undercover III* which have sold over half a million copies.

He can be contacted at: mk_emka@yahoo.com.

Also by Moammar Emka:

published by Monsoon Books
Jakarta Undercover

published by GagasMedia, Jakarta
Jakarta Undercover (Indonesian edition)
Jakarta Undercover II (Indonesian edition)
Jakarta Undercover III (Indonesian edition)
Red Diary
Ade Ape dengan Mak Erot
Tentang Dia
Siti Madonna
265 Days, 3 Lovers, 2 Affairs
Beib, Aku Sakau

JAKARTA
UNDERCOVER II

MOAMMAR EMKA

monsoon

monsoonbooks

Published in 2007
by Monsoon Books Pte Ltd
52 Telok Blangah Road
#03-05 Telok Blangah House
Singapore 098829
www.monsoonbooks.com.sg

ISBN: 978-981-05-9109-0

Copyright © Moammar Emka, 2007

The moral right of the author has been asserted.
All rights reserved. No part of this publication may be
reproduced, stored in a retrieval system, or transmitted,
in any form or by any means without the prior written
permission of the publisher, nor be otherwise circulated
in any form of binding or cover other than that in which
it is published and without a similar condition being
imposed on the subsequent purchaser.

The names of the people and places written here have been changed or
initialled to protect privacy. If in some places original names of people
and places have been used, it was for the sole purpose of writing the
book, not to disgrace the aforementioned.

Cover photograph copyright © Black Studio / Collin Patrick
www.black.com.sg

Printed in Singapore

12 11 10 09 08   2 3 4 5 6 7 8 9

Dedicated to those who firmly believe in safe sex.

Contents

Foreword

I never thought that *Jakarta Undercover* would be so warmly welcomed by readers. I am grateful and lucky that, through my book, I finally got the chance to speak to so many people. For me, the conversations I had were both surprising and shocking because they were conversations about sex and sexuality. Such themes are taboo for many people and some people were uncomfortable talking to me about such things.

So it is true that experience is the greatest teacher of all. I learnt many insightful facts from having so many conversations with so many different people, such as the general public, college students and intellectuals.

Once, I was invited to Yogyakarta and engaged in hot debates with institutions such as Gajah Mada University (UGM) and Institut Agama Islam Negeri (IAIN) Sunan Kalijaga. I also went to other cities where I visited Diponegoro University (UNDIP) Semarang, Satya Wacana University Salatiga, Airlangga University (UNAIR) Surabaya, Parahyangan University (UNPAR) Bandung, Bandung Islamic University (UNISBA), Jember University (UNEJ) as well as some bookshops like Gramedia and Toga Mas. In all these places I experienced many interesting things and was asked many intriguing questions: What's the reason behind publishing *Jakarta Undercover*? Why do you choose to write about sex? Why do you expose in detail the one thing which is still taboo for many people? Aren't you afraid that people might use your book as a sex guide, which will be a negative influence on society?

I was asked most of these questions when I went on talk shows on several college campuses around Jakarta, such as Indonesia University (UI), Atmajaya University and Universitas Islam Negeri (UIN), which used to be IAIN Syarif Hidayatullah, my alma mater for the four years I was at college. I tried to explain to people that by writing *Jakarta Undercover* I was simply trying to inform my readers about the reality of the sex industry in Indonesia.

So why sex? Because it is a subject no one talks about and, as I recall, at that time there wasn't any other book which explored Jakarta's sex industry so directly. Nowadays there are more and more books tackling this subject. That's why I thought sex would be such an interesting subject to write about. It is like a strange alien which intrigues everyone but most people are too shy to admit it.

If the book was later used by some as a sex guide, that's up to the reader. I tried my best to disguise all the names and places and, besides, the aim of the book was to explore the issue of the sex industry, not to promote sex itself. None of the chapters contain a sex scene, and anyone who has read my book will know that.

Another interesting point to make is that several of the questions I was asked related to my religious background: Why is it that, given your religious background and after studying religion for several years, you end up writing about sex? Isn't it a contradiction?' These were common questions I was asked, and touched on the behaviour of the middle classes and the idea of women as objects.

For me, some of these questions started me thinking. To be honest, it was my religious background that made me want to know more about the nightlife around me, nightlife I had never experienced before. The world I knew when I studied at schools with a strong Islamic background—such as Madrasah Ibtidaiyah (MI), Madrasah Tsanawiyah (MTs), Madrasah Aliyah (MA) and IAIN—was like a white screen which always showed the same old faces.

It was the world of journalism which opened my eyes to black screens, and I have to admit that I was tempted to find out more. The result was my book, which I really hope can help anyone who reads it. At least it will open people's eyes to the reality of the sex industry, and encourage people to come up with solutions for making our world better. It's a cliché, I know, but that's how I feel. If we can first talk about sex without feeling embarrassed, then we can begin to find some common ground to solve the problems together.

The black screen wasn't always frightening. There were other sides which showed the good side of humanity. During my research I encountered many female sex workers, and not every one of them was doing it for the money—some were doing it to fight for something greater. Take Vonnie, for example. She's a massage girl who also offers sex services for between Rp500,000 (US$60) and Rp1 million (US$120). She does it so she can pay for her child's medical expenses. He suffers from Down's Syndrome and even though he is six years old, he has the mental age of a baby. Then there is Lina. She was just seventeen years old when her parents sold her into the sex industry. And Lusi, who is forty years old and works as a mammi. She has been a single parent for many years and does it to take care of her three children.

Another criticism I received was that I used 'I' in my stories: Why does every story have the word 'I' in it when you were never involved in the situation, only watching? Isn't that a bit hypocritical?

Even my friends, the actress Rieke Dyah Pitaloka and writer Ayu Utami, jokingly said that using 'I' made people think one of three things: maybe 'I' was a homosexual because he never seemed tempted by hot exotic dancers; maybe 'I' was impotent; or maybe 'I' was so religious that nothing could tempt him away from his faith.

I blushed when I heard this, and replied that their theories were not even close. I tried to explain that the 'I' figure only seemed like an observer but in reality he participated in those events too. For example, when 'I' refused to have sex with the beautiful girl inside the shaking Pajero, it was just for sake of the plot and the setting. There were times when the 'I' figure had to be the actor and times when he had to be the director. Many times I had no choice but to take part. In *Naked Clubbing,* the first requirement to get inside the party was to strip naked, so I had no choice but to strip. It was basic logic: How could I write about a nude party if I'd never even been to one?

I was asked similar questions when I went on radio talk shows in Jakarta and other cities: HRFM, Cosmopolitan FM, I Radio, MTV On Sky, Prambors, Female, U FM, S Radio, Radio One, M97 FM, Smart FM in Jakarta, Colours, I Pro 2 FM and Suara Surabaya in Surabaya, Trijaya and Sonora in Yogyakarta, Mas FM in Malang, OZ Radio, Ardan, 99FM, Rase FM, MGT and HRFM in Bandung. Or when I was the guest star on several TV chat shows like Halaman Depan and Sensual in Trans TV, Selamat Datang Pagi in RCTI, Love and Life and Midnight Live in Metro TV. Or when I went on several infotainments like Kabar-Kabari,

Cek dan Ricek in RCTI, KISS in Indosiar, 99per cent and Kroscek in Trans TV, Inside Celebrities in TV7, Hot Shot and Poster in SCTV, MB on TV and Jumpa Pers in Lativi and also GO Show and Celebrity Update in TPI, which broadcast every single day.

However, when I was invited as a key speaker on Midnight Live on Metro TV in September 2003, something surprised me. The show was on for one hour and for that whole hour I exposed Jakarta's nightlife. During the interactive session the station received at least 800 SMSs, 400 callers and the computers crashed. For me that proved how interested people are in finding out the truth about Jakarta's nightlife. Even though I knew I would be criticised, I felt it was important for me to speak to the public. That's how you hear different viewpoints and learn from your mistakes. I managed to answer some of the questions, but others I had to look into first. All in all it was a very positive experience.

That's why I decided to write a sequel to *Jakarta Undercover*. As you probably know, the events written about in the first book are just a small part of what really goes on in Jakarta's nightlife. There is a lot more.

I have spent almost six years studying the nightlife in Indonesia. Some call it 'the grey world' or 'the illicit world', and I uncovered so much that I knew it wouldn't fit into just one book. So I wrote *Jakarta Undercover II* to complete the first book, which focussed on the sexual behaviour of the middle classes and high society. The main themes of the first book were about how exclusive nightclubs provide sex menus as the main course, and how the middle classes and high society are used to free sex. But I think the second book shows that the sex industry also operates among the lower classes.

I hope that *Jakarta Undercover II* will answer the questions and criticisms I received for the first book. But then again, maybe not, which is why I ask you to please tell me what is on your mind. The reader is the author's best friend when it comes to criticism.

Unlike *Jakarta Undercover*, eighty per cent of what is inside this sequel has never before been published. The remaining twenty per cent has appeared in several magazines like *Male Emporium* (ME) and *Djakarta*.

Lastly, this book was published with the support and help of so many people, and for that I would like to thank you all.

First and foremost, thank you to Allah SWT for letting me live my life, be alive on His earth and for every blessing he has given me.

Next I would like to thank my parents, abah H. Markun and ummi H. Musri'ah, my brothers Muflihah, the late Minhaj and Mahfufah and my little sisters Nafisah and Mutammimah, who are always there to support me, no matter what.

For my best friends: Aip Leurima, thank you jaz; Jamer 'Tong Clay' Siahaan, thanks, bro; Chris Luhulima, Kiki Susilo, thanks, co; Dodi Tri Widodo, thanks, Mr Lecturer; Cornelia Agatha, thanks, darling; Echa-Kum-Kum, thanks, beb; Sonny Lalwani, Rizal Mantovani, Abdee and his SLANK; Bebi Romeo & Tommy F Awuy, thank you my man, thank you bro; and also Garin Nugroho, *matur suwun yo*, Mas (thank you so much, Mas). Also to Desmond J. Mahesa, thank you for everything, bro.

To Susy 'Sisi' Harlianti, thank you so much for such a lovely afternoon tea. When I remember it I always laugh, think seriously, then laugh again.

For Hermawan Kertajaya with his Mark Plus, thank you for the marketing buzz.

To Ria Irawan, Aa Izzur, Teuku Ryan, Audy, Anya Dwinov, Vira Yuniar, Novia Ardana, Dewi, Ricky Jo (my bro), Vicky Burki, Jose Purnomo, Lusy Rahmawati, Meisya Siregar, Happy Salma and Edi Brokoli, thank you for your support, smiles and laughter.

To my dear beloved friends at GagasMedia & AgroMedia: Boss Anton, Boss Andi, Kang Hikmat, Kang Tanudi and also Mas Julius (Galang Press), Pak Johan and Mas Arif Toga Mas. I deeply appreciate your hard work in keeping my book in the market.

I can't forget the Menteng gang and Gardu gang: Pak Rey & Devy, dik Miko, Lisa, Didit, *'tante'* April, Risa *'yayang'*, (de) Silvi, Mas Eko, Dedi Batak, (Pra) Susi, Popy, Melly Zamri, Jo Marcela, Ane J Coto, Gugun Gondrong, You Die, Weny, Wisnu *'nyo'*, Wisnu Andhika, Luftan, Lena, Little Boy, Big Boy, Morie, Satria, Dina, Nirmala, Erwin, Richard, Edwin Abeng & Ririn, Jimmy, Reta, Dina 'Chris' and so many more that I can't mention every one. You're the best and all the best ...

Thank you to Bang Paul and Bang Fritz for their valuable lessons on how to define life. To 'neng' Ussy Sulistyawati, Jane Shalimar, Trie and Tasya, good luck in reaching your dreams, girls.

Also to my writer colleagues: FX Rudy Gunawan, Richard Oh, Djenar Maesa Ayu, Ayu Utami, Nova RIyanti Yusuf, Sitok Srengenge and Fira Basuki. I gratefully thank you for all your meaningful, casual discussions.

To Boutique 21 Gang Plaza Senayan: Herlan, ANce. To some of my best buddies who became members: Grace, Fett, Oge, Riri, Tejo 'TTC', Edy Bogel, Peggy and the rest of the gang who would sit for hours just to share stories with me and laugh. Thanks a lot.

My deepest gratitude to the late Pak Mujimanto Asmotaruno and friends at *Male Emporium* (Cintya, Dede, and Andriza), and I-Radio (Rafiq, Tony and Untung D). Also my thanks to my gang in Indigo (Pak Will, Ardy, Chris, Agung, and Ludy) who gave me the chance to do the lifestyle coverage for SILET in RCTI.

Thank you to Heriyadi H. Sobiran, the chief of *Popular Magazine* who was always there when I needed someone to talk to. Also to Dono Baswardono, Mas Dadi Darmadi who was struggling through Harvard University, Baby Jim Aditya, Bung Gege and Mammi Di and also some names that would made the list even longer if I mention them all.

Last but not least, to my fellow press who I deeply thank for the role they played in promoting *Jakarta Undercover* not only nationwide but also worldwide. I can only give you my humble gratitude for all your support.

The Central
Asian Blue Sauna

There are many top exclusive fitness centres in Jakarta which serve not only local 'talent' but are now starting to add Central Asian ladies to their menus.

Everything began with a harmless idea—an idea that came from Chandra. Chandra is a thirty-five-year-old lad who runs an advertising agency at Gatot Subroto. He challenged our friend Riko to a little adventure with these Central Asian ladies.

It was after hours at the Hard Rock Café in Thamrin, Jakarta Pusat, and the three of us—me, Riko and Chandra—had accidentally gathered there after Riko, who had just finished his regular workout at a fitness centre in Menteng, suggested it. Luckily Chandra and I were nearby when Riko called us. It seemed like a good idea to gather somewhere and wait until rush hour and the traffic jams had passed. Anyone knows that at this time—around 5.30 pm—it is impossible to go anywhere by car. Chandra lives in Bintaro, and Riko in Cibubur, so they had two choices: get stuck in traffic jams trying to get home at such a crazy hour, or have a few beers somewhere first until the traffic cleared.

'Let's have beers! I don't want to grow old driving in such heavy traffic!' said Chandra once he'd arrived and joined our table. Riko appeared ten minutes later, still dressed in his sports gear.

'I want an OBS. What are you guys having? Beers?' Chandra asked. OBS is a drink made up of thirteen different kinds of alcohol. You can find it in almost every bar and club in Jakarta. OBS stands for Orang Bisa Senang (Make People Happy), and is Chandra's favourite.

'Beers,' we replied.

A waitress came to take our order. It was still early and the place was almost empty. Smooth background music played as the evening drew in and Jakarta's sky turned from red to black.

'Do you or do you not want to know more about the Central Asian ladies at MS Sauna?' I asked, suddenly remembering that Chandra had bragged about them several times before.

'There's no way we could invite them here. Are you crazy? It's better if we just go there. I don't lie about things like that,' Chandra answered.

So one hour later we left the Hard Rock Café to see if what Chandra had told us was true. None of us wanted it to be just a lie.

'You guys go ahead,' I said. 'I'll catch up later. I swear, I'll come.' I had to excuse myself since I had to do a one-hour broadcast at a radio station first.

'Make sure you come or it will be your loss,' Riko said.

We said goodbye at the car park. Riko decided he would leave his car there and travel with Chandra, who was still driving his beloved black Terano.

I arrived at MS Sauna at 9 pm. When I called Chandra he said that they were waiting for me at the karaoke room, so I parked my car in front of MS's luxurious building. MS was certainly the biggest and most sophisticated building there. This four-storey shophouse complex—which officially offered saunas, shiatsu massages and a karaoke/home theatre—was located opposite the supermarket.

I rushed into the karaoke room. Two female receptionists gave me a warm welcome. I glanced around and saw that the lobby-cum-restaurant was quite full that night. When there were a lot of people queuing for the facilities, the restaurant doubled up as a waiting room or was simply used as a hangout, decorated with beautiful waitresses.

A girl escorted me to the second-floor karaoke room where Chandra and Riko were.

'What took you so long?' Chandra yelled at me the minute I arrived.

I ignored him as I surveyed my new surroundings. I'd initially thought MS was another discotheque, club or bar with a restaurant and karaoke setup. In actual fact it was more like a fitness and relaxation centre. The room was a bit dark but I could make out a big screen on the wall in the centre of the room. The song 'My Way' had just finished playing and 'No Me Ames' followed. I could see that Chandra and Riko were sitting comfortably on a black sofa. On the table was a bottle of Jack Daniel's, a few glasses of coke, an ice bucket and a few small fruit platters. Suddenly I got it: they were planning on being here for quite sometime and could hardly wait for the real 'main course' to arrive. Chandra looked like he was more than ready for it.

'Where are the girls? Are you guys into each other? This is totally lame. It sucks, man!' I laughed.

'Easy boy, easy. We're waiting for you,' Riko said.

I pointed out that I was only interested in Central Asian female escorts since the locals were getting too common. Without any more small talk, Chandra and Riko called to the waitress.

'No need to worry about that. We can order one each. C'mon, Chandra, order now!' said Riko and we all laughed.

Chandra left the room first. He knew Jakarta's nightlife inside out and he was well connected, having access to key people in many of the city's entertainment hot spots. MS was no exception.

Ten minutes later he came back to his seat with a big smile on his face. It was the kind of smile I knew only too well and had only seen on occasions like this. Chandra drained his glass of JD on the rocks, then poured himself another. He asked me and Riko to make a toast.

After several slow songs and a few more drinks, a lady entered our room. She was neatly dressed in a suit, and I guessed she was in her forties. A badge was pinned to the right side of her jacket with the name Lili written on it. She gave us a friendly greeting.

'Mister Chandra, would you prefer to see the display room or for me to bring the girls in here?' Lili turned out to be the coordinator for the ladies. She told us that the foreign girls were mainly from Uzbekistan, the Philippines and Thailand. She said there were also three from Tajikistan and two from Russia.

'Maybe I'll just bring the ladies here then,' said Lili.

'Yup, that's a great idea, Mammi Li. We'd prefer Uzbeks, Tajikistanis and Russians,' Riko replied immediately. Mammi is the word for a female pimp and this one certainly was a big mama.

I began to take notice of where I was. The home theatre-cum-karaoke room had only sofas and a table with a small bathroom off to one side of it. I wondered how this room could be love-spree arena when it didn't even have a bedroom.

'We're not having the love spree here, buddy. It's on the third floor. The three of us will have a sauna or shiatsu massage upstairs. Get it?' Riko explained, as though reading my mind. Oh, silly me. Of course, upstairs. I suddenly realised our karaoke room was just where we picked the girls and the services we required.

By then it was already 9.45 pm, and coming to our room were five Uzbek girls, two Tajikistanis and two Russians. They stood in front of us, smiling broadly, and started to introduce themselves. For me, that was a truly amazing moment because they were all so gorgeous. I have never seen such beauty before. They were all so pretty and their bodies were so hot, super sexy. I didn't know which were Uzbek, Russian or Tajikistani because they all looked so similar. Even the way they spoke sounded the same. I kept asking Riko which one was from where, but he reminded me that the most important thing was that these ladies were Central Asian.

'It doesn't matter which one is Uzbek, Tajikistani or Russian. They are all so pretty. Just pick the one you like best,' added Chandra.

Then I set my eyes on one girl. She was so beautiful with dark hair that made her look even more attractive. She was tall, probably around 170 cm, and her body was plump and not too flat. Chandra and Riko were more into the blondes. The girl I picked said her name was Zena and her other friends were Alisa and Yala. Zena said she came from the land of Lenin while Alisa and Yala were from Uzbekistan.

After talking to her for quite a while I realised that she not only had beautiful dark hair, but also full tempting lips. I really liked the way she talked, smiled and was friendly. Alisa was a natural blonde, very tall and slender with eyes like almonds. Her face was oval and she had thin lips painted with sexy red lipstick. Yala, the blonde girl, was not as tall as Alisa but her body was as sexy as Zena's—a bit plump but still sexy. The V-neck tight T-shirt she was wearing made her look like a total knockout. Sex appeal emanated from her, teasing every man who set eyes on her. Zena also looked super sexy, with her tight jeans and short

T-shirt showing her beautiful belly. We decided to take things slowly and hang out with the girls for a while in the karaoke room before hitting the sauna room. I noticed that all three of them were speaking English with a strange accent, which made it a bit hard for us to really understand what they were saying.

But that was the thing about the karaoke room—conversation wasn't really a priority. So we just sang some songs and drank. It was so funny and amazing to see how such beautiful people like them could be so tone deaf. Zena picked 'Zombie' by The Cranberries and sang it twice, while Yala was desperately trying to sing 'Desperado'. They both failed dismally.

Blue Sauna, Blue Shiatsu

Slowly but surely the temperature was rising. We toasted several times, laughed and talked, even though we hardly understood each other. Less then one hour later the alcohol started to take effect. Our faces began to turn red and our stomachs were getting warmer. The girls' faces were starting to turn red as well. That was when Chandra and Riko thought it was the perfect time to go to the shiatsu room.

'I'm getting high. Think I'd better go to the shiatsu room,' Riko said and grabbed Yala by the hand. They both took off. The rest of us left a couple of minutes later. Riko had been right. If we'd stayed in the karaoke room for much longer, we probably would've got really drunk. When I looked at my Guess watch it was 10.15 pm.

'I can't stay too long. You know how my wife is. She goes mad if I get home really late.' This was why Chandra wanted us to move on to the next service. He'd been married for four years and had a kid.

Chandra booked us a VIP room on the first floor. This was where the shiatsu and sauna treatment took place. It had quite a big sauna pool, but not the kind that we could all use at the same time—this one was more private. Then I realised that only VIP rooms had private saunas, a treat for guests who wanted 'special' treatment. Inside our VIP room was a long hall, aisles and other smaller rooms. Chandra and Riko each took rooms that were practically next door to each other, while mine was the one in the middle of the hall. There was a number written on a small board hanging above the door.

My VIP room was quite big. It had a bed, two chairs and a dressing table. The dressing table had a mirror and big drawers which contained sheets, a kimono and some towels. There was also a bathroom with a small sauna inside it. The air-con inside the VIP room was supposed to keep it cool but the hot steam from the sauna in the bathroom was making the entire room hot.

Zena took care of everything. She made the bed and put the towels and kimono on the table. She took her time. She even lit a cigarette and sat on a chair while I lay on the bed. Soft music began to fill the room from a speaker on the wall.

'How about taking a bath first?' Zena asked in a tempting voice. Unfortunately her English was very confusing so she had to make gestures with her hands to make me understand what she was saying. Then she circled her hand around mine and walked me to the sauna in the bathroom. In the blink of an eye she undressed me, hung up all my clothes then undressed herself.

The party had officially started. In the sauna Zena acted like an expert babysitter bathing a baby with tenderness and care. She herself was not totally immersed in the water, using a white towel to cover her body, but she still took the lead. She rubbed, massaged and touched my back softly, sometimes pinching my body sexily. Oh my god, that fifteen-minute sauna was beyond words.

'Okay, now dry yourself, then you can relax on the bed.' Zena gave the commands and I obeyed wholeheartedly.

Now it was time for the shiatsu massage. In reality, however, it was not really a traditional shiatsu massage since the word 'massage' was just another word for sex. For this treatment Zena had already prepared a condom, one that she'd brought herself. She told me she always uses her own condoms—never ones from guests, and not even from MS's office boy who sells condoms on the side. I suppose she feels more comfortable and safer bringing her own.

'No condom, no sex!' Those were her exact words. 'For me, safe sex is a must. Not only is it dangerous not to wear one, but it's not going to be cheap either when you fall ill.' And this policy of only using condoms she'd brought herself applied to oral sex too. This girl was very well informed about STDs.

The sex dates that Zena and her Central Asian girls offer are similar to other services that girls in most massage parlours offer. The only difference is that Zena and her girls massage the genitalia rather than body muscles, as with a traditional massage. But, of course, these girls do not come all the way to Jakarta just to be paid the same as their local competitors. They are highlighted on the menu and are more expensive because they are different. A VIP sauna plus shiatsu-massage-sex treatment costs about Rp2 million (US$240). That is a minimum estimate based on Rp1.5 million (US$180) for Zena and the rest for renting the room. But the aforementioned price does not including the cost of food and drinks. Chivaz, vodka and Black Label drinks can cost between Rp600,000 (US$70) and Rp700,000 (US$85). And if you are a tipper, it's possible to add another Rp300,000 (US$36) or more to your bill. If you decide to go with a local girl you can spend at least Rp1 million (US$120), including the room rent.

So all in all it's quite expensive. Nonetheless, MS is never short of customers. They are open from 2 pm until 11 pm every day. The guests keep coming, craving the selection of girls from Eastern Europe, the Philippines, China and, of course, Indonesia, all of them with their pretty faces and killer bodies. Beds and saunas are the only witnesses.

Afternoon Sex
with China Girls

For those who are into China girls or like to try younger women, some popular massage parlours are open from midday till late afternoon. It's heaven on earth.

It was around midday when I drove to a place around Monas. I'd been woken from my nap by a call from my friend Ronny. He's such an impulsive guy and likes doing things spontaneously. His offer was too tempting to ignore, so I decided to go with him to the TSC Club.

Ronny is my other clubbing mate. At least three times a week we hang out together after work, have afternoon tea or go to the hippest discotheques. But there are times, like that day, when his naughty devilish urge takes us on a love spree. Two nights before, we'd been to BC Bar at Thamrin. We spent the whole night partying until suddenly, at 2 am, Ronny made me go to a karaoke club at Kelapa Gading.

'My friends are there. They want to do karaoke but they've also hired a stripper. C'mon, let's join them—and I don't take no for an answer,' he insisted. So off we went and ended up staying there until 5 am.

Afternoon Sex

At around 2 pm were were driving towards Mangga Besar (Mabes). I'd met Ronny a while before at Thamrin. We decided to leave my car at Sarinah's car park and instead use Ronny's pride and joy, his black Cherokee.

Ronny is slim, in his thirties, with straight hair. He's married but claims to be separated. He works around Fatmawati, Jakarta Selatan, dealing in cars and spare parts. When we met that day he was wearing his usual casual clothes: a T-shirt, a pair of jeans and a pair of trainers. Ronny opened his car window and called out to me to join him. I finished my cigarette and hopped in.

'Where are we going?' I asked.

'TSC Club. I went there a couple of months ago.' Ronny accelerated, almost as though he was scared that the club would vanish if we didn't get there as soon as possible. From Thamrin we went straight to Mabes. Ronny was craving for a massage parlour that was busy and open twenty-four hours a day. TSC is quite well known among guys who desperately need to relieve their biological urges.

When we got near to Mabes we went to a certain area called LKSR. The huge complex is popular among people from Jakarta because you can find almost everything there: different kinds of shops, discotheques, massage parlours, saunas, beauty salons, hotels and shopping malls. It was not hard to find TSC since we had been there before. It is located within a huge shopping mall, so we went straight to the mall's car park and parked Ronny's car in front of a karaoke discotheque.

'Do you know which way to go? I forget,' I said because it had been quite a while since I'd been there.

'We just take those stairs to the first floor,' Ronny replied. 'How can you forget?'

When we reached the top of the staircase we saw the entrance to TSC. In fact, TSC is not really a massage parlour. I would say it is more a café or restaurant. The main room looks exactly like a café with a small stage, a bar and seductive lighting. No matter how strong the sun is outside, inside TSC it always seems like night-time. Disco music reverberated around the whole place while waitresses were busy serving guests. We picked a spot in the corner, not far from the bar. That afternoon the place was quite full. Judging from what we could see, it was not only full but full with girls. The girls certainly outnumbered the men.

'One Long Island and one beer, please,' Ronny asked the waiter dressed in a purple uniform. He then turned to me. 'Let's relax a bit. That way we can see which girls are the best.' He practically had to yell into my ear because the music was so loud.

At the corner just near the entrance were the girls who were still 'available'. They were sitting in groups talking, sometimes flirting with the guests, whilst the ones who already had their clients were busy entertaining them. Mammies (lady pimps) were busy selling their commodities. That was the selection process. A couple of minutes passed by and a band began to play on the stage in front. They sang their first song and by the time they had finished, a mammi was coming toward us.

But first I have to tell you more about TSC. What is so special about this place compared to similar massage parlours is that it is open at the unusual hours of midday until 9 pm. This is quite early compared to most massage parlours which operate during the evenings, or even twenty-four hours, and reach their peak between 11 pm and midnight. If you visit TSC in the evening, you won't get such a good selection of girls and the atmosphere is not as thrilling as it is in the afternoon. Having different operating hours to the other massage parlours is quite a good idea as it gives TSC a distinctive edge, making it a very successful business and one of the hottest spots for love sprees.

Of course, the operating hours are just one small part of what makes the place famous and always full—the menu also has a lot to do with it. The club is known for providing China girls and younger girls. You can either browse as you please, or simply order from the mammi. She makes sure you get exactly what you wish for.

'Bet you want a Chinese lady with big boobs, 36B. I know you always dig those girls, ha ha,' Ronny laughed. 'I think you know my type as well, right?'

'China girl for sure,' I said.

'You know me too well,' Ronny laughed again.

China Girls

It was getting crowded inside TSC when the mammi brought us our girls. We'd decided to use the mammi as we are both quite practical: why bother to browse, squinting in the dark, turning left and right to find a girl when mammi knows best, right?

The first girl introduced herself as Alin and the second girl was called Yenny. Alin was in her early twenties with quite a slender body, long straight dark hair and small eyes. Yenny was a bit plump and not very tall. She had round eyes and wavy brown hair. Alin was exactly what Ronny had asked for, definitely China bred, while Yenny admitted that she had been born and raised in Jakarta.

Alin told us that she had been working at TSC for about nine months with Mammi San as her pimp. On the other hand, Yenny claimed to be a freelancer. TSC had several freelancers but they still had to have a mammi in order to work there. There were three mammies at TSC, each taking charge of at least twenty-five girls.

'You won't be disappointed with Alin or Yenny, trust me,' Mammi San whispered to us, trying to convince us how great her protégés were. Mammies always want to make sure that the customer won't change his mind and ask for another girl. They are good at marketing, these mammies. They are all experts when it comes to sweet-talking customers.

'Would you like another drink?' Alin tried to break the ice by smiling sweetly and offering us more drinks. She looked like she was a friendly girl, and her shyness turned Ronny on.

'Could I have a Black Label and coke?' Yenny asked spontaneously. Alin ordered one for herself too, her favourite drink.

The band on the stage was still performing, playing the requested songs. For the next fifteen minutes the four of us chatted and drank. That was when Alin told us her story about never having the chance to visit her home country, China, because she'd been born and raised in Jakarta where her parents ran a small shop. Yenny told us stories about how she'd tried her luck at advertising, music videos and TV dramas. Several times she'd got lucky and once she'd been offered a small part in a TV drama. Even though it had been a small role, she was very proud of it.

'Well, you can't blame a girl for trying, can you? The most important thing is that I get to experience a lot of different things,' added Yenny, who worked at TSC three or four times a week as a freelancer.

While we were chatting it became obvious that Ronny was getting comfortable with Alin, and he wanted to see some action. So they both left. There were two doors: one led to the toilets and the other to ten or fifteen other rooms where the action took place. Alin led Ronny to one of the other rooms.

'When it's too crowded we have to wait for a sign from Mammi before we can go through,' Yenny explained to me. I've heard that on Saturdays and Sundays, when it's completely full, guests have to wait quite a long time for a room to become available. Luckily for us we didn't need to wait that long.

On the outside TSC is not really anything special, just another place which caters to the flourishing sex trade. The reason why people go crazy for it is that its menu offers girls from China and younger girls. Plus it is affordable for any guy who has an income of at least Rp2 million (US$240) a month.

'The room rent costs Rp50,000 (US$6) and you pay the cashier directly. As for the girls, you pay Rp200,000 (US$24) for each girl, not including tips,' Yenny informed me frankly. So in order to get a date with a girl at TSC it would cost you between Rp400,000 (US$48) and Rp500,000 (US$60). That's including food and drink because there is no way you can just sit there doing nothing while you are both waiting for the room. And if your girl is a heavy drinker, watch out guys!

'Let's go inside.' Yenny took my hand and teased me with a sensual smile.

The afternoon flew by. Most people would rather spend their afternoon in a cosy shopping mall with a lovely cup of tea or coffee. At TSC it is another world. Most of the guys there are busy getting some action in the arms of a sexy China girl—a lovely afternoon of sex.

After Lunch Striptease and Hand-Roll Services

There is one club which caters to working men. Exotic dancers perform in a private room right after lunch. It is what they call one hell of a 'dessert'.

'Sex after lunch' is also called BBS, which is short for Bobo Bobo Siang. *Bobo* is an Indonesian word for sleep, and *siang* means noon. So *bobo siang* means taking a nap but, of course, in this case it is nap time with strong hand gestures. BBS is becoming common among executives in Jakarta, not only with men but also with women. The truth is that sex after lunch no longer means having a secret affair with a colleague and going to a hotel room for sex at lunchtime. Now it involves making regular journeys to love-spree places during the lunch hour.

It is no secret that these places are almost everywhere in Jakarta. Some are even located inside office buildings, blending in among the companies. Some are even next door to them.

It is no wonder that love-spree places have finally showed their faces in public areas. As I said before, they are everywhere, on every corner. Just walk straight and you'll find a strip club, turn left and you'll see a massage parlour with extra services, make a U-turn and you'll find karaoke bars with their more-than-willing female escorts waiting to give you maximum sexual pleasure. And not every love-spree place is open at night; some of them open during the day. Even though night-time is still the most popular, these daytime places still have a lot of guests. They are making Jakarta even hotter than it already is. In one private room guys sweat through their lunch.

KB Club is one such place you can go for sex after lunch. When lunchtime comes around some men enjoy desirable meals in the company of strippers. The selection of food is amazing—from local to Western, it is your call. But what is more amazing is what the strippers do to their guests during the lunch. The menu is absolutely crazy: oral sex, hand service, hand roll and intercourse.

Mixed Services

KB Club is famous for one-stop entertainment. It's a billiards bar, café, music lounge and karaoke club all in one. It first opened in 1997 and later became famous as a café. It has been lively ever since.

Personally I love the place. I can spend hours there playing billiards or relaxing in the lounge, café or karaoke club. For these past two years I always make sure I spend time there. Sometimes I just got here to hang out with friends, play billiards till late at night or just enjoy the live music which is always amazing. On every night out—Wednesdays, Fridays and Saturdays—KB Club is the perfect pre-party place or meeting point before you hit the other discotheques.

When night falls the billiard arena is full of men and women playing and laughing between disco beats. There are more than forty tables, and the waiters and waitresses are usually quite busy. The room glows from the lighting above the billiard table. It is the kind of place where everybody seems to be having fun, or at least trying to. The café is next to the lobby. There is a stage there and a band play regularly. On week nights the crowd is not as good as it is on Friday and Saturday nights.

On the second floor there is a music lounge. It is the best place to go to relax and have intimate chats with spouses or friends as cosy music lights up your night. The place is so cosy that it is full every single night. But the music lounge is also the rendezvous point for a guy to meet up with his female escort. Sometimes they only meet for a casual chat and a few drinks and karaoke. Sometimes it is more than that.

One night I was hanging out with my two friends at KB's music lounge. Raymond is thirty-three and Zack is twenty-eight. I have known them for quite a while and we hang out at KB Club a lot. Most of the time we play billiards until it is time for us to go clubbing. Sometimes we place bets to make it more interesting. Another thing I like about the KB Club is that is it never boring.

This particular night, sometime in late January 2003, we didn't feel like playing billiards, so we decided to go to the third floor for karaoke. We settled our bill and headed to the exit next to the bar. The exit is covered with a long black curtain and when it is drawn you can see a huge lobby where two receptionists smile at every guest. To the left of the reception area is a VIP billiards arena, and to the right is a small stage with a live band.

'Are we going to stop by the café first?' asked Zack.

'We can't really hit on anything at the café though. It's pointless. Let's just go for karaoke,' Raymond replied.

Day and Night Strippers

We went to the third floor via a set of metal stairs. It was a bit dark and the DJ was still playing music to liven up the place. We were asked to wait for a moment in the lounge while a waiter prepared our karaoke room. We didn't mind at all because we got to watch the beautiful female escorts who were making the lounge more interesting. Not long after that, our karaoke room was ready.

We entered a long hall with music blaring from the rooms on either side. The walls were all painted blue and there were doors on the right and left sides of the hall. Each room was named after a different music genre and the one we had was named Classic Rock.

'Please enjoy yourself. Pak Kus will be here shortly,' said the waiter. Pak Kus (Mr Kus) is the assistant manager at KB but the day-to-day running of the karaoke rooms is not the only thing he is in charge of. On the side he is also a papi (pimp) for several female escorts and strippers. He has worked at the club for more than three years.

Pak Kus has a real talent for picking the right girls for his clients. He has a good eye for these things and good taste as well. A guest is usually left in the lounge for a few moments so he can pick the female escort he desires, or he can pick a girl straightaway from the karaoke room. The pimp in charge brings between five and ten female escorts or strippers to the room. They strike their best pose for a few minutes, then let themselves out. The guest then tells the pimp his choice, which is then relayed to the girl.

We waited for fifteen minutes, drinking and singing songs. Then we ordered more drinks and food: vodka orange, beers and some snacks. The Classic Rock room is just like any other karaoke room: adjustable lighting, a long sofa for ten to twenty people, two coffee tables, a twenty-nine-inch TV with two microphones and a sound system by the wall.

'Good evening, gentlemen.' Pak Kus greeted us from the door. 'Icha and Lita are ready.'

'Please send them in,' Raymond requested.

Icha and Lita appeared at the door with a friendly smile across their faces. Lita was wearing a tight little black dress. She was twenty-five and had short hair and fair skin. Icha was tall, around 168 cm, and a bit plump, with medium-length hair. She wore a miniskirt and a grey tank top with a leather jacket over the top. I thought she was around twenty-five as well and she also had fair skin. They both had on make-up and the scent of their bodies screamed sexy.

'Hi, Ray, long time no see. Where have you been?' Icha immediately gave Ray a warm welcome. She walked up to him and without any hesitation sat on his lap like a little girl who'd missed her daddy so much. Lita sat on the sofa. We engaged in the usual small talk for another ten to fifteen minutes before it was time for the girls to take over.

Around 9.10 pm Icha and Lita finally went into the bathroom to change their clothes. 'Let's get started, but first we need to change,' Icha teased us from the bathroom. All of us could hardly concentrate on the song we were trying to sing in the karaoke room. Then it was show time! Icha and Lita emerged dressed in skimpy outfits which hardly covered their bodies. The lights dimmed and the TV screen that had been playing karaoke videos suddenly started showing a sensational show where naked girls danced erotically. Then the music started. Icha and Lita began moving sexily, taking off what little fabric was left on their bodies until they were both completely naked. Seductively they started to approach us. Icha threw herself at Raymond, teasing him with her body. Lita joined in and approached Zack. Suddenly they were both teasing us all, not only swinging their hips and breasts but touching us in all the right places. Then it was time for them to strip us too. Icha sat on Raymond again and starting to open his pants. Lita did the same to Zack and me. For a stripper, this was the point when a lot of tips could be made. The dance itself took no longer than twenty minutes, and the rest was just seductive foreplay. Sometimes they pinched, squeezed or kissed us. The size of their tip was their real goal at this stage.

'Don't be shy,' said Icha, who was sitting naked on Raymond's lap and unbuttoning his shirt. Raymond looked cool, but it was obvious he was so turned on.

'I surrender. Do what you please,' said Raymond.

'But you won't forget the tips, will you, Beb?'

'Of course not.'

Then she started to give Raymond a range of other services: oral sex, hand service and hand-roll service. Lita did us too. It was the routine. Sometimes, after dancing, these girls would even have sexual intercourse with their guests. The hand-roll service, which has become the trademark of the strippers at the KB Club, is actually a hand job. Imagine a basketball player when he rolls his basketball on court. The hand-roll service also reminds me of a Japanese dish where seaweed, rice, fish eggs and vegetables are rolled together into a long slim tube.

After two hours in the karaoke room we decided to leave.

'Let's go guys,' Raymond said when we finished paying all the bills. 'Let's go clubbing.' He finished his vodka orange. Icha looked excited. She and Lita had put their clothes back on but their bodies still smelt so irresistible.

'Why don't you take us?' Icha pretended to get mad.

'We'll let you know when we decide,' Raymond replied with a big grin on his face.

'Just make sure your mobile phone is on,' Zack said.

'We'll make sure of that,' said the girls. That was when I saw the bill: Rp2.3 million (US$280) rental for the karaoke room for three hours (the minimum is Rp625,000 or US$75), food and beverages totalled Rp975,000 (US$118) and entertainment (the strippers) came to Rp700,000 (US$85). Of course that did not include the several hundred thousand rupiah we'd given the girls in tips. The hand-roll service usually costs at least Rp200,000 (US$24).

On the way to the car park we passed some karaoke rooms where the action was still taking place. We stopped in front of the door of one of the rooms and smiled to each other, trying to figure out what was going on inside. We figured they were enjoying what we'd just enjoyed.

'I wonder what they are doing inside,' said Zack.

'Maybe one of them is being ... you know ... "karaoked",' Raymond laughed and we all joined in.

Later I found out that, during the day, KB Club is also full of men who wish to swop the heat outside for a different kind of heat inside. During lunchtime the place is practically full because it is located near to the business district and office buildings. A lot of executives have their lunch there. Of course they don't just order an ordinary lunch, but the kind of lunch that makes you sweat—really sweat.

Sex and Tripping Heaven—The Three-Night Party

A luxurious nightclub with the coolest dance floor was offering extra excitement with additional lust trips on each floor. The sound of the disco was so loud on the fourth floor that you could actually feel it with every beat of your heart. There were hundreds of partygoers dancing nonstop, as if tonight was their last night. It was 4 am and yet there was not a single sign that this party would end soon.

My head was a bit heavy and I was feeling sleepy. I'd got there three hours earlier at around 1 am. I was beginning to wonder when this party would draw to a close. I tried to stay awake by drinking beers. One beer after another was how I survived.

'You want to wait till the party is over?' Benny, my clubbing mate, seemed to read my mind.

'No way, man. They won't stop until Monday morning or noon,' I replied.

'They are all on ecstasy. If you aren't going to take a pill, you'd better go home now,' Benny added.

It was not like I didn't know that already. It was so obvious that most of them were high, using ecstasy to boost their energy till the party was finally over. But what I couldn't really understand was how they could stay here three nights in a row. To me that was unbelievably mad!

'Ben, let's go to the third floor and see some live music. I heard there are lots of pretty ladies there. I get bored here.'

'It's closed now. Better we come back again next week,' Benny replied.

And so we did. The next weekend we went back to SD Club. We arrived at around 11 pm. For the past three years SD Club has been the 'it' place for party people in Jakarta. It is a one-stop entertainment hub which has turned into a temple of party mania in Jakarta. People gather here from every corner of Jakarta and party three nights in a row.

The very first time I came to SD was two years ago. That time I didn't really explore the place, so when I heard rumours that the club was able to offer lots of extra services, I decided to find out for myself.

SD Club is so famous that it is a piece of cake to locate the place. From the main junction near Kota we made a U-turn, then turned right. In front of us was a huge building which was always busy. Near to SD Club there are lots of massage parlours and discotheques, which add to the late-night entertainment value of the area. When we arrived the car park was almost full and the valet hardly got a break. Sexy ladies, some waiting for a car, stood in front of the entrance smiling.

After giving our key to the valet, we slowly walked up to the building. I noticed that there were several hawker places around the club, and they were also full of customers, mostly couples. Five minutes later we entered the building. The first thing we saw was a restaurant full of diners. The lighting in the restaurant was so dim that some of the couples were able to make out or talk intimately without drawing too much attention to themselves. Next to the restaurant was the billiards arena, which was also quite full.

'Let's go upstairs. Nothing special here,' Benny said.

'But this is a good spot if you want to really talk to your date, isn't it?' I argued as we walked towards the lift. Actually, every service that SD provides on every level is nothing new for me. Being a one-stop entertainment hub, the club has a huge variety of entertainment on every floor. On the second floor there are karaoke rooms and saunas. Of course, that's not anything new or special. It is just another floor for karaoke and sauna with female escorts and strippers. You can find it almost everywhere in Jakarta.

'If you want a private party, you just book the suite. It's bigger and cosier,' Benny added while smoking his cigarette.

On the third floor is the live-music lounge which has a live music performance every night from 10 pm till 1 am. This is where most of the beautiful ladies hang out. It looks a bit like a harem since there are so many women here, and what is so great about this music lounge is that almost every woman here is ready for a quickie or a one-night stand. These ladies are here to find a customer, to tease the men, and when the men are interested the mammi or papi takes over and seals the deal.

Next to the music lounge are standard three-star hotel rooms, ready to be rented. One thing you can be sure of is that here, a short-time transaction is much cheaper than those on offer outside.

'Many people call it the "super deal". For only Rp300,000 (US$36), you get yourself some fast love,' said Benny.

When we finally went to the fourth floor it was already 1 am. As always the music beat so hard my heart pounded and the dance floor was full. It was dark, but every so often colourful lasers would sweep the entire room. This was where everybody came to enjoy heaven on earth. I walked around the room with Benny and everywhere I looked people were lost in the music, shaking as if their bodies were controlled by the beat or some outside force. Some were shaking their whole bodies, while others were just moving their heads, lost in their own worlds. A few people stayed seated, moving so slightly that it was difficult to notice their movements.

SD Club is famous for its Three Day Parties. From Friday till Monday morning or noon, the club is open nonstop. It was amazing how many people never tired of partying for three nights in a row. This heaven-on-earth ecstasy is what drives them to search for more excitement. They are always craving for the instant high that ecstasy gives to their world. Also known as Inex, the drug has many names and comes in many different colours. Some call it Black Heart, or Playboy (because it has a picture of a playboy bunny on its top side), or Optic, and so on. Some say that the best types are Black Heart and Optic, which can cause a certain kind of hunger afterwards. A standard pill costs around Rp100,000 (US$12), whereas a Black Heart pill can cost around Rp300,000 (US$36) to Rp400,000 (US$48). It never fails to amaze me how something so small can have such a dazzling effect on someone.

Dawn Sex

Finally we ended up at the bar. In front of the bar there was a long sofa with lots of pretty ladies sitting on it.

'Hello, gentlemen, care to look at my new girls?' An old lady came to greet us. She was a mammi, and she was not the first mammi who'd tried to hook us up with girls that night. As soon as we sat at the bar another mammi immediately called out to her protégés and the selection process began. Some of the girls were standing near to the bar while others were sitting on the sofas. They were the ones offering fast love. On the fourth floor, the price you have to pay for this excitement is less than it is on the third floor, plus the fourth floor is open till 5 am while the third floor closes at 2 am.

The mammi introduced her protégés one by one. They all looked pretty in their miniskirts, tight jeans or sexy fitted outfits. But the mammi was very good at reading our faces—she just knew when we weren't interested, and would quickly put another girl in front of us. We picked a few girls and they tried to make conversation, but it was pointless as the music was so loud.

In the other corners of the room it was the same script, different cast, as girls tried to make small talk with their clients. Some couples had already taken it one step further by going to the fifth floor, also known also as the four-and-a-half floor since there was no lift to take you there, only stairs. On this special floor was the place where all the action took place. Clients could choose from different kinds of rooms, standard to VIP.

'What are we going to do now? Karaoke, massage or would you rather trip?' Benny asked me.

'Hm ... let me think about it. Karaoke is closed, and I don't think I can cope with the three-night party. Let's just have a massage for a couple of hours,' I said.

To get onto the fifth floor at this time of night we had to use the emergency stairs near the reception desk. The stairs near the dance floor were only open from noon until 2 am, and it was already 5 am. It was indeed an emergency situation. Soon we reached the fifth floor. There was a huge hall with lots of rooms along each side.

'Which room would you prefer, sir?' A middle-aged woman greeted us. She was the cashier-cum-receptionist. 'We have VIP and standard rooms. The VIP room costs Rp275,000 (US$33) and the standard is Rp250,000 (US$30).'

The price was, of course, for the room and the girl. All payments are made to the cashier and they accept cash and major credit cards. Of course, when it comes to the tip it all depends what is going on inside the room. For those who prefer safe sex, the staff can easily order condoms.

The VIP room we went into was more like a room in a three- or four-star hotel, only smaller. There was a twenty-four-inch TV with audio system for karaoke. It also had a long sofa, a small table and a bed with white sheets and a bed cover. A wall-sized mirror was to one side of the bed so you could practically see yourself in action!

'Do you want to clean up first or are you ready for some action?' Mercy, the girl I had hired, was only twenty-three years old. She had fair skin, shoulder-length hair and came from Subang. She guided me to the shower so I could clean up a bit first, then she joined me in the shower, splashing warm water all over her body. Afterwards she covered herself in a white towel and lay on the bed.

Then it was time for foreplay: sexy massages (seductively pressing my whole body with her fingers), oral sex and a tongue-licking bath. The full service came last but not least. That morning was like watching a one-hour drama on TV—one which had a happy ending. I'm not sure who was happier though. Maybe Mercy because she got more allowance, or maybe some of the guys in the next room, guys who finally succeeded in expressing their desires and fantasies instead of going crazy by keeping them locked inside their heads.

Mount Blow
Service and Loly Thai

It was a service offering oral sex but the Macau girls sure took it to a whole new level.

'I come from Macau and I have been working here for six months. I like Indonesian men, they are all so nice. They are never rude, always polite.' And that was coming from a very fine girl indeed. She had fair skin that looked as soft as milk, an oval face, sexy thin lips, a slender figure and long, straight hair. Her name was Amoy. The night I met her she was relaxing on a sofa at one of the many love-spree places we'd visited. Her English was not fluent, but the way she ate a fruit platter was so adorable that we didn't really pay much attention to the way she spoke.

'I like working here. But as you may notice I don't speak English very well so it is a bit hard for me to communicate. I love talking to people, sharing stories and stuff, so this is my biggest challenge.' The words kept coming out of her small mouth, and she was the one who was doing all the talking.

That night at the CI Club, four of us were in a karaoke room: me, my friend Doni, his 'date' Loly (a Thai girl) and, of course, Amoy. The small talk stopped a moment later. It seemed like Amoy realised that I was finding it very difficult to understand every word that she was saying. Like most Chinese people speaking English, she had a strong accent that made her English unintelligible. She spoke Mandarin well but Mandarin is not a common language in Indonesia. She had learnt some Indonesian words, but she'd only got as far as 'thank you', 'good night' and 'good afternoon'. The karaoke songs Amoy chose were also in Mandarin, which we didn't really like because we couldn't understand them. She tried to sing Indonesian songs but she only knew two.

'I have to master at least one or two Indonesian songs. So I learnt. But I only know two,' Amoy admitted when we asked her how she knew the lyrics to the song she was singing. It was one of Indonesia's biggest hits, a song by Nike Ardilla, a famous Indonesian singer who died a decade ago at the peak of her career in a car crash. The song was called 'Bintang Kehidupan' ('Star of Life') and even though Amoy knew the lyrics well, she still sounded weird singing in Indonesian.

Meanwhile Doni, who was sitting not far from me, was busy with Loly, trying to make every minute spent with her worth his money. Loly was one of the stars at the CI Club. She was so pretty and looked like a model. Her body language was as hot as her sexy outfit. It was no wonder she was one of the highest paid girls there. It came down to the cold hard reality of economics: supply and demand.

A couple of minutes later Doni took off with Loly to their private room. I waved them goodbye and smiled. That left only me and Amoy in the karaoke room. She moved towards me. 'Do you want to start now also?' she whispered to me. I nodded and she pushed a white button on the wall to call a waiter. He came in and Amoy ordered something. While waiting, I sang a Dangdut song called 'Benang Biru' by Meggy Z. When the song finished the waiter came back with two mugs. The first mug contained warm ginseng tea, the second was water with ice cubes. This is the 'mount blow' service that everyone has been talking about. It is oral sex using ginseng tea and cold water. First Amoy drank the warm tea. Then, when it was almost time to climax, she immediately drank the cold water and ... well, the rest was just mind-boggling.

I wasn't expecting the traffic light to turn red. I had to brake immediately which sent me straight back to earth with a bang. I'd been thinking about the night Amoy had given me the most unforgettable oral sex. Now it was 9 pm and I was on my way to CI Club to meet my friend Leo. That was probably why my mind had charged off uncontrollably, remembering my experience two months before. I told myself to concentrate on the road.

You remember the CI Club, don't you? Let me refresh your memory.

The CI Club is one of the clubs renowned for having ladies from Uzbekistan and Russia. Nowadays it is also famous for two other special services that many guys find very amusing.

This was going to be my fifth time at the CI Club. My friend Leo—a thirty-three-year-old businessman who was involved in the import and export of electronic goods—hadn't been back for nearly two months and he'd begun to miss the routine there. For the last few months the CI Club had been the most talked about place for a love spree. It was because the club kept introducing new services that thrilled adventurous guys. Clients kept coming back and asking for one, two and even three of the short-time services they offered.

The Three-Sex Service

At 10 pm I arrived at CI Club and headed straight to the Chinese restaurant which had become part of the club. I was supposed to meet Leo there. The club itself isn't very difficult to find as it is located in one of the business districts between two famous banks. In Kota and Mangga Besar, CI Club is one of the most exclusive clubs to go to. The place is always busy, day and night.

I spotted Leo sitting at one of the tables. He was waving to me. I approached him and sat down. He seemed to be distracted. I followed his gaze and noticed a group of girls sitting in the other corner of the restaurant. The girls were all wearing sexy outfits and looking their best, a sure way to market girls in a place like this.

We moved to the karaoke room which was not far from the Chinese restaurant, next to the entrance to the discotheque. A receptionist welcomed us and showed us to a room. It was a VIP room with a twenty-nine-inch TV and a four-star bedroom with en suite bathroom. The air-con made the room so cool and nice.

We each ordered a Jack Daniel's with coke and ice, some snacks and fruit platters. A mammi came to our room but there was no small talk; she simply showed us what was on the menu. The CI club has ten mammies and all of them are middle-aged women dressed in formal suits. The first thing the mammi offered us was a striptease dancer who was either local or foreign, it was up to us. Most guys choose local girls because they are cheaper but have the same sensational impact as imported ladies. For one show a local girl costs Rp350,000 (US$42), while a Filipino or Thai girl can cost around Rp1 million (US$120) for one show. These ladies are more than just dancers. As long as the price is right they are more than willing to make your dreams come true. And it is through these jobs on the side that strippers make a lot of money—it costs from Rp500,000 (US$60) to Rp1 million (US$120) for fast love.

Next the mammi offered us the option of a female escort. Again, we were shown a selection of girls based on their origin: local, Taiwanese, Filipina or Chinese. And yes, almost every one of them was available for any kind of service. However, the most popular service is still the mount blow service, as mentioned before. To order this with a girl from Macau costs around Rp1.5 million (US$180). After introducing clients to the menu, a mammi usually then brings out her protégés for the guests to select. Mammies play a major role in the business of love sprees and they make a lot of money. One time I asked a mammi how much she made. 'We get at least twenty-five per cent from every deal,' she replied.

Then we were offered a date with an imported lady, typically from Uzbekistan or Russia. Sometimes the club has girls from Spain or America but they are ordered specially. Girls from the Philippines, China and Taiwan are also imported. Nowadays it is considered trendy to date an imported girl, something the CI Club pioneered. This is another reason why the CI Club is so popular among love-spree maniacs: they are considered trendsetters in this business. A word of warning though— never raise your expectations too high. Imported ladies do not dance as well as strippers. They tend to just drag the guy to bed, but they are absolutely professional and make a three-hour date well worth your money.

The mammi then told us that for a girl from the third menu it would cost around Rp3.5 million (US$420) for three hours. This meant that for three hours in a karaoke room, a girl would be your most desirable companion and the date would end in bed for sure.

If you want to book an imported girl outside the CI Club, that can also be arranged. However, this service is strictly limited to guest members or loyal customers that the club knows well.

As well as twenty-four-hour karaoke and services, CI Club is also famous for its hip discotheque, which reverberates house music almost every night. At weekends the dance floor is so crowded you can't even move, and ecstasy is not only complimentary but essential to making the party merrier. On special occasions the discotheque holds special events: Lingerie Show, The Lingerie Queen and Clubbers' Party. Famous DJs light up the night along with a live show from sexy dancers.

Hottest Club,
Nude Hostess

The club's motto is: ALL YOU CAN GET, ALL YOU CAN EAT. *It is the biggest and most glamorous new place in Jakarta and the next big thing for relaxation. Here you can treat yourself with all-round luxurious services. The menu offers a range of delights, from tasty cuisines to sinfully delicious, sexy Chinese girls.*

'What type of room would you like, sir?' asked Tina, the receptionist, dressed in a baby-blue uniform.

'Just deluxe, please,' I said.

'Would you like karaoke or would you prefer the massage and spa treatment?' she asked again.

'Massage and spa.'

'Have you booked the massage girl, sir?'

I shook my head. 'From the car park I came straight here and you are the first person I've seen.' I smiled at her and she smiled back.

'Sure, no problem. The GRO (Guest Relations Officer) will take you to the display room and you can select a girl, sir. We have plenty: locals, *cungkok*, even *bule* are available.' Tina explained all this to me in detail as if she was at a business meeting presenting a new product that she was trying to convince me to buy. She spoke very well and looked very professional. It was as if she was the public relations officer of the club, giving specific details on the club's services. Oh, by the way, *bule* is an informal Indonesian word for Caucasian, whilst *cungkok* is ... well, you'd better read on to find out.

My conversation with Tina did not take place at some hotel or meeting room, but rather at the newest, hippest love spree place in town. Since the CG Club had opened about six to eight months before, everyone had been talking about it, which was the main reason why I was there that night. Some of my friends had said good things about the place, which was supposed to be the biggest and most luxurious nightclub in Jakarta. It covers an area of more than one hectare and offers almost every service a man can dream of. Its relaxation and entertainment services are guaranteed to banish stress.

It was just too bad that my friends were all busy that night, so instead I'd come by myself. Some were busy dating their girlfriends, some were going out with their wives, while the rest were having family dinners at home. So there I was, alone, a single man ready to kill my Saturday night at CG.

CG is very easy to find because it is located in the densest business district in Jakarta. All I had to do was drive straight from Sudirman to Jakarta Kota until I reached Glodok. When I found the trade centre with shophouses on both sides, I made a U-turn. Thirty metres from there I turned left and entered the big trade-centre complex which not only contains electronic shops but also cafés, restaurants, pubs and discotheques.

The Presidential Suite

After parking my car in front of CG's building I took the lift to the third floor. That was where I met Tina. On the third floor there is a health club, a spa and a massage service, but you can find the same service on the fifth floor too.

Tina introduced me to Yanty, a GRO, who led me to the display room. The room was no different to a showroom or a shop window. It had a glass wall behind which the girls were exhibited.

'Would you prefer a local girl or a *cungkok*, sir?' asked Yanty.

'I think a *cungkok* would be great. Are they more expensive?'

'Of course,' Yanty laughed politely. 'Imported girls are slightly more expensive than locals, sir.'

'Ok, no problem.'

Then Yanty led me to another display room which had at least thirty girls on show. They were all *cungkok*, an informal word for Chinese girls. Actually I could have easily booked one from the room I'd rented, but I preferred to do it this way. It gave me many more options. But alas, the more girls I saw, the more confused I became. They all looked the same to me. They were almost all the same height and size, and even their faces looked similar. Finally I gave up and asked Yanty to pick one for me, a friendly and chatty one.

Yanty appeared with a girl named Caroline. She was not too lean, had nice fair skin and straight, shoulder-length hair. That night Caroline was wearing a sexy green sack dress and heels. She looked so elegant. To look at, you would never think she was a nightclub hostess.

On the way back to my rented room I noticed that there were a lot of rooms clustered around the health club and spa area. The interior was very rich and the equipment was all very modern. You could shape and tone your body in there and feel sophisticated at the same time. There was a sauna room, a steam bath and pools of different temperatures that you could take a dip in. When I finally entered my deluxe room it reminded me of a four-star hotel room. On that floor alone the club has about fifty of these luxurious rooms to rent for massages and spas. The deluxe room I'd rented had a whirlpool and a bed. Caroline, my date for the night, immediately took care of everything. She made the bed and prepared the towels.

Some of the boys who'd been to CG Club before said that either the massage girl or the hostess could offer a 'nude service', meaning that the entire massage session would be clothes free. This nude service costs around Rp750,000 (US$90), including the room fee, food and beverage. But if you think it just goes that far, think again. If it is fast love you are after, it can be yours, as long as the price is right. You simply negotiate directly with the girl you have hired.

'Usually it won't cost you more than Rp1 million (US$120),' said Heru, one of my friends who has been to CG three times. To be honest, it is absolutely impossible to relax in such a cosy room while a naked girl is giving you a body massage. No wonder it usually ends in sex.

'Two people of the opposite sex, naked and alone in one hell of a comfy, air-conditioned room. It would be such a waste to just freeze in there. You'd end up getting sick,' Heru added. That was when he told me his story about the nude massage at CG.

When the one-hour nude massage ended, I went back to the receptionist and told her I was curious about the other services they had to offer. I wanted to know what has made this place so popular that it has become the coolest one-stop sex-tainment hub in Jakarta. Yanty then let me browse around the presidential suite. I was speechless. It is enormous and well facilitated too, having the capacity to hold up to fifty people. In the middle of the room there are two plush sofas and three big screens. Off to one side is a dining room with two televisions, complete with local and foreign channels. It has a splendid bedroom, a shower cubicle and a private DJ area. The DJ area has direct access to the discotheque area located at the main hall. This can hold up to 3,000 guests. It is crazy! And it even has twelve balconies around the discotheque for special guests who wish to dance privately with their group without having to mingle with the other guests on the dance floor.

Back in the presidential suite there is also a mini bar, a sofa, a sauna and a whirlpool. It also has a room for aqua therapy which contains a bathtub, a twenty-one-inch TV, a café corner, a massage sofa and a big screen. Can you imagine that? I could throw myself a private party right in that room. Everything would be so well prepared: food, drinks and girls. It would be absolutely perfect.

'A lot of high-profile people, commissioners and businessmen usually book this presidential suite for private parties,' said Yanty.

After my breathtaking tour of the presidential suite, Yanty showed me the other facilities that CG had to offer. It was evident from my tour that this place has everything. Yanty showed me a live-music lounge which can hold up to a hundred people. In the middle of the lounge there is a fountain with an exotic statue of a dragon. The club also has a wine cellar for those who fancy wine and cigars, and there are a lot of thematic karaoke rooms, ranging from standard, to superior, to VIP, to suites. The rooms are named according to the interior decor or theme. For example one room is called Submarine because its interior resembles a submarine. It has a dining table, attached bathroom and can hold between ten and fifteen people. Another room has an oriental theme. Another is a suite with a gazebo inside, a dining table, an en suite bathroom and a very private relaxation room which can fit almost thirty people. Every karaoke room has two big-screen TVs with remote controls so the guests can operate everything automatically.

'You can get it all here, everything you want.' Yanty emphasised the words 'everything' and 'all' as if she could read my mind and sense my amazement.

It was gone 10 pm when I left the CG Club and headed for Gardu, a billiards place around Taman Ria Senayan. By then I was more than ready to join my friends for another round of clubbing. After all, the night was still young ...

Erotic Nurses Party, Topless Girls and Sexy Boy Dancers

Party, party, and party! Yup, the word is so familiar to the cool people who make up Jakarta's nightlife. In Indonesian we called these partygoers anak gaul. *They can be found in big cities in Indonesia, especially Jakarta, a city where parties light up the metropolitan night.*

Parties take place not only in public places such as cafés or discotheques, but also in private houses, apartments and villas. And a party is not complete without a dazzling theme. One café once held a party where everyone had to wear the same colour clothes, such as Red Party or Black Party. Other specific themes include Wet Party, Gay Party, Ladies Night Party, Bubble Party, Wild Party, Lingerie Party and so on.

Then there is a party which uses dancers as party magnets. In most clubs the dancers even become the mascot of the party to attract guests. They come up with different themes each day and the trends keep changing. The places which offer live shows can come up with really bizarre ideas.

The Erotic Nurses Party

Early in August 2003 there was a hot party called the Erotic Nurses Party. Of course it didn't involve the kind of nurses you'd find in a real hospital but rather the kind of sexy nurses you see in triple-X-rated movies. That was the theme of the party, with sexy dancers dressed up in nurses' uniforms.

Picture this: at 1.30 am the music is really loud and the place is full of people dancing and drinking alcohol. Suddenly three girls all dressed in nurses outfits hop onto the bar top and start shaking their bodies sexily, teasing everyone who sets eyes on them. The temperature begins to rise. For a few moments all eyes are on these sexy nurses, who have now started to take off their uniforms, leaving only scant items of clothing to cover their private parts. As the alcohol keeps flowing, the atmosphere heats up.

That was the first time I saw strippers in public. Usually I paid for them in a private karaoke room, but this time it was at a club called BR in Thamrin which was fast becoming one of the hottest spots for Jakarta's party people. It was a breakthrough event because not many places had the guts to host such a sensual live performance in public.

BR Café is located on the first floor of a shopping mall and only open on Wednesdays, Fridays, Saturdays and special occasions. For me, BR is nothing new. Like most partygoers in Jakarta, I am a regular visitor. I often go there on Friday or Saturday nights. BR—which is known for its RnB, trance and hip-hop DJs—is quite popular among youngsters in Jakarta, so it is never dull, especially at weekends. Youngsters are the club's biggest customers, but there are also quite a few executives who are big fans too.

BR is not too big. It is located in the centre of the room with a dance floor surrounding it. There is a small stage designed especially for people who like to dance on top of it. Above the dance floor is a dining room whose interior is completely metallic.

The night of the Erotic Nurses Party, three dancers dressed as nurses suddenly appeared wearing black veils. The crowd was stunned. The three dancers began to dance sexily. One of them was smoking a cigarette and sexily blew smoke into the audience. I had to stop myself dancing so I could really pay attention to what was happening.

Time went so fast. The girls were all almost naked now, with only their genitals covered. The crowd was going crazy, screaming hysterically, which added to the thrill of the atmosphere. The erotic live show lasted for about half an hour, and had a huge impact on the clubbers who were being driven by the music.

After the sexy nurses left, some of the guests got really bold and started dancing on the bar. The bartenders were getting really busy pouring drinks one after another, and the night was getting even hotter.

The idea of having erotic dancers dressed as nurses was terrific yet unique. Usually at these kinds of parties the dancers only wear extremely sexy outfits and tease the audience with their sexy moves. There's never really any action, not like there was with the nurses. They really stunned the audience, and the crowd was still there until gone 3 am.

What made the nurse action so great was the element of surprise. That night none of us were really expecting to see a sensual live show. Better still it was a striptease performance from girls in nurses uniforms. How cool is that? I looked at my invitation again and noticed that all that was written was: EROTIC NURSE DANCER, nothing more. That was why the crowd had stayed at BR for so long, even though it was getting really crowded and hot—you literally couldn't move. Most people left when the music stopped and the party was over.

'It would be such a waste if I leave early. When will I ever be so lucky again as to see half-naked sexy dancers like that in front of so many people?' said Arman, a twenty-six year old who'd come with his three male friends. I must admit I also left BR late that night, afraid I'd miss another sweet surprise such as the erotic nurse dancers.

The Topless Girls

On September 2003 the BR Club threw another wild party. It was a huge event to celebrate its third anniversary. I remember it was the biggest party of the month. By 11 pm hundreds of guests had filled the club. Early in the evening we watched several live performances from famous singers, then there were games with lots of door prizes to give away. For almost two hours, six famous MCs, dancers and singers entertained us with their talents.

At 1 am the party, which was full of famous faces, was starting to heat up. It was heating up because it was so crowded, and also because the female guests had been drinking and were starting to dance uncontrollably. Free-flowing alcohol fuelled the dancing. Standing on top of the bar, the bartenders kept pouring alcohol into open mouths on the dance floor. Some couples on the dance floor completely lost control and started to get busy with each other. Some were spotted kissing, some were in the middle of deep kissing and some, shamelessly, were engaged in a little foreplay. Again the ladies started to get wild. Some hopped onto the bar counter and began to dance wildly, taking off their skirts and showing off their G-strings. Some began to dance sexily while taking off their bras and giggling. Of course these scenes were warmly welcomed by the male guests, who were also screaming and cheering wildly.

At 2 am five girls suddenly stood up on the bar. They were all wearing tightly fitted sexy black outfits. The five girls, who all had lean sexy bodies, started to heat up the club with their killer dance routine. Slowly but surely and in a most seductive way, they started to take off their tops until they were all dancing topless. The crowd cheered even more. Impatient guests began yelling at them to take off their bottoms as well.

'C'mon! Take it off, take it off ...' they yelled over the loud music.

The girls ignored their cries and even teased the audience more. Sometimes one of the girls would act like she was going to take off her bottoms, but then after a while she would adjust it back in its proper place. This act of teasing was driving the audience absolutely crazy. But still, the girls never took off their bottoms.

As the girls began picking up their tops from the bar counter and putting them back on, one topless dancer entertained the crowd. Then all five of them disappeared to the changing room and the crowd cheered loudly. Then the guests who were drunk hopped onto the bar and starting to dance wildly, releasing their inner sensuality. The party finally ended at 4 am. Some people went home, while others hopped to the next club that was open twenty-four hours and the party continued.

The Sexy Sex Show

Both the Exotic Nurses Party and Topless Girls Party are only two examples of the kinds of parties that make Jakarta's nightlife thrilling.

The truth is that there are a lot of discotheques and clubs which hold similar events where dancers strip in front of hundreds of guests. A lot of parties have themes with special appearances from models wearing sheer lingerie or wet clothes, or dressed in bikinis or going topless on stage—all to spice up Jakarta's nightlife.

Another party I recall was in mid-February 2003 when I visited one of the clubs located in Kota, Jakarta Barat. A club at Jalan Hayam Wuruk was holding a special event in its discotheque. The event was called In Bed With Marilyn Monroe. Eight models walked on the stage topless, each of them using a wig to try to disguise herself as Marilyn Monroe. The choreography of the show was not bad at all. The models walked like professional catwalk models. In the centre of the stage there was a sofa and a girl dressed as a queen was sitting on it. Her outfit was so sheer that everyone could see right through it.

Afterwards the strippers took over the stage. They weren't exactly on the stage but rather danced inside a huge golden cage. One by one girls entered the cage until there were four of them dancing erotically together. For it to be a striptease show they had to remove their clothes so, slowly but surely, they took off what they were wearing until they were all completely naked. As if being naked was not enough, they then started to act. Sometimes they would mimick two lovers passionately making love, another time they pretended to be tigers ready to fight. Colourful spotlights followed their every move, making the night even more sensational. The action lasted about twenty minutes, then the four of them vanished and the club went completely dark. Loud house music still blasted out.

I noticed that CI's discotheque was so modern. It was laid out as half a circle, with a stage in the centre of the room and a dance floor right in front of the stage. On both sides of the stage there were tables. The DJ area was across from the stage, and on one side was a special spot with comfortable sofas. In front of that were two sets of stairs leading to the first floor where the VIP rooms were. The entrance to the VIP area was guarded by three or four security guards and separated by a silver metal fence. The stairs were covered with a red carpet. I took my time examining the VIP area. Luckily for me several of my friends were having a party at that time. The VIP area looked a bit like a balcony because from there you had the best view of the stage and the dance floor.

I went up to the VIP area for about ten minutes, then I went back to the dance floor, which was still full of people dancing around. The lights came on again. Inside the cage there were two naked dancers. Dancing on a flight of stairs nearby were two more naked dancers. They were using veils to cover their faces, which was quite a sight. Each girl was exposing her entire body, using only a small piece fabric to cover her face! The lights followed every move the dancers made. Suddenly everyone in the room was focusing on them.

'I thought they were only go-go dancers, but it turns out they are completely naked! Wow!' commented Erik, who was sitting at a nearby table with two male friends and a girl.

The Boy and Couple Dancers

It seems like sexy male dancers also want to be a part of Jakarta's nightlife. I've watched the boys in action on several occasions, both at private birthday parties and in clubs, cafés and discotheques.

In June 2003 I attended two events. Sexy male dancers were the highlight of both. The first event took place inside a four-star hotel around Sudirman. TPK Café is usually full of female customers aged twenty-five and over, so it's no wonder male dancers often perform there.

I'd come because I'd been invited by the dancers' coordinator. His name was Agus and he was twenty-nine years old. He had a big sturdy body which suggested that he worked out a lot in the gym. I met him at UT Café in Kuningan. It is a café that is well known as a hangout for girls who are into *bule* (Caucasian) men. I go there sometimes just to spend time or enjoy their live music. So when I met Agus for the second time he—along with two of his friends who also looked like body builders—invited me to TPK Café.

'You should come. I'll bring my dancers. It's a fashion and dance event. It's going to be great. You have to come,' said Agus as he handed me four invitations. Each invitation admitted two people. The event was taking place on Friday, 13th from 9 pm onwards.

So I went. It was around 10 pm when I got there. The café was already crowded with guests. There was a huge stage in the middle of the room which was covered with a big white screen. When I arrived a band were performing live on the stage, singing popular local and foreign songs. There were two vocalists: one male and the other female. Their duet was awesome, but something else caught my eye. The place was almost entirely full of female guests, with only a handful of guys sitting in groups on the right side of the stage. I decided to sit in the corner nearest the bar. From there I had a good view of all the action. After he'd finished briefing his dancers and before the show began, Agus approached me.

'You came! Thank you. How come you didn't bring anyone with you?' he greeted me.

'They've all gone to Embassy or CO2, as usual,' I replied.

'The show is going to start soon. Why don't you have a drink first? Or, if you have the guts, why don't you pay a visit to those ladies who are sitting right in front of the stage?' I turned my head to see where he was pointing to. Near the stage there was a table of five ladies, all in their thirties and all loyal customers of TPK Café. Agus told me that these ladies were all into younger men. Before I could find out more, Agus disappeared backstage to get his dancers ready for the performance.

At 10.30 pm the lights suddenly went out and the room fell silent. Smoke filled the air and the music started again, but this time it was really loud. Through the smoke on the stage, five guys appeared and the stage lights were switched on again. The lights followed the guys, exposing their every move. They were all wearing sheer, tightly fitting T-shirts so you could see their torsos, and super-tight pants exposed their private areas. All five of them had athletic bodies, the kind that women dream of.

Everyone began to clap hysterically in time with the music. The way the male strippers moved was no different to the way female strippers move, but I have to admit that not all of them could dance very well. There were two who looked a bit robotic, but with bodies like theirs I doubt the women even noticed—especially when they started taking their T-shirts off. When the female guests began applauding loudly and screaming wildly, the dancers became even more enthusiastic. Some of the ladies even began to mimic their sexy moves. After almost half an hour the male dancers and their sweaty bodies had truly heated up the room.

I found the same scene when I visited PO Café at Jalan ISK-Blok M Jakarta Selatan. The event took place in late June 2003, when my friend Lucy invited me to a birthday celebration. Lucy, a widower with two children, owned her own restaurant and ran a boutique. She was thirty-eight years old and was always busy. She took part in arisan and dance classes, would hang out in malls and cafés, and once or twice a year she would hold charity events to raise money for a local foster home. For her thirty-eighth birthday Lucy booked the entire PO Café and threw a private party. Only people who had been invited to her party were allowed inside the café. (PO Café is not very big, maybe half the size of the Hard Rock Café in Jakarta.)

Around 8 pm the guests started to show up and we were invited to help ourselves to the delicious food and beverages that were on offer. The café had also prepared several shows for Lucy's party. There were performances by a DJ, percussion player and many famous singers who sang one or two songs for her. But the highlight of the evening was, of course, the super sexy male dancers. Each one wore only a *cawet* (a tight male thong) to cover his penis. As most of Lucy's guests were female, they enjoyed the performance immensely. Some smiled, some screamed wildly and some went bananas, laughing till they cried. But that was the alcohol talking, I'm sure. Ever since we'd all set foot inside the café, the alcohol had flowed.

Lucy admitted that hiring sexy male dancers to light up her party had been her idea. She said that she and her girlfriends had been to one or two private parties where male dancers had performed.

'But tonight is different because there are a lot of guests. It's just to make the party more fun, that's all. Everyone can sit back and enjoy almost-naked guys. Isn't that extraordinary?' said Lucy, who was wearing a black backless gown.

'Why don't you have female strippers?' I enquired.

'I have a lot of female guests. It's not much fun for them to watch female strippers,' she replied.

'Then why don't you have couples? Boys and girls?'

'Just wait and see. Soon I'm going throw an even bigger and crazier party!' She sipped a glass of red wine, her favourite drink.

Hiring sexy male dancers to perform is not only popular at private parties like Lucy's. Several cafés in Jakarta are starting to offer this service too, such as JL Café at Kuningan, SN Café around Sudirman, GG Café around Kota, HI Discotheque near Ancol and many more.

There are also a couple of dancers that everybody has been talking about who perform on the third floor of ST Discotheque in Kota, Jakarta Barat. When ST Discotheque threw its seventh-anniversary bash, as well as lining up DJs there was also a performance by a couple who stripped and danced topless. It was similar to the shows put on in nightclubs in Kings Cross, Australia. Couples perform on stage, witnessed by hundreds of people. Even thought the show at ST Discotheque wasn't as vulgar as those in Kings Cross, it was still pretty wild. Both dancers covered only their private parts and moved like two people having sex. Sometimes the guy was lying down and the girl was sitting on top of him, then they would change positions. Their skin was covered with oil so that it shone beautifully when the lights came on. They also had heavy make-up on their faces; black for the guy and different colours for the girl.

'It's totally crazy by Jakarta's standards, even though the couple are not completely naked,' commented Rio, a twenty-five-year-old guest that night.

Family Management

One important thing I've noticed with regards to love sprees is the issue of family involvement. Do you remember the three dancers from the Erotic Nurses Party? I was shocked to discover that these three girls— whose names are Rima, Linda and Angel—are actually managed by a middle-aged woman who is the mother of one of the girls! I met them the afternoon before the show, during their rehearsals. Luckily I knew the event organiser, Raka, who is thirty-seven years old. He helped me to get to know the girls better.

When I met Rima, Linda and Angel they were wearing their casual clothes and they looked like average youngsters you would find hanging out in malls or cafés. They were with a middle-aged woman who was wearing a white shirt and black trousers. All three girls looked quite similar. I later found out that the woman was forty-nine years old and called Mrs Taty. She was the one managing the girls.

Out of the three of them, Rima was the one that I found to be the most friendly. This girl with wavy, long hair was really nice and we got along instantly. Without any hesitation Rima introduced Mrs Taty as her mother. To tell you the truth I was horrified. Her own mother was managing her schedule. Unbelievable.

'Mama takes care of everything for us, from dealing the price, organising the legal documents and other stuff,' said Rima matter-of-factly. She told me she had been born and raised in Jakarta. Her mother was from Menado and her father was Chinese. Linda and Angel were also related.

When it came to dancing, Rima's mother was a lot more experienced as she'd also been a dancer in her youth. Whereas Rima was a topless dancer, her mother had been a snake dancer. During the 1980s snake dancing had been hugely popular. At that time almost every nightclub offered a snake dancer as the highlight of the evening.

What was even more interesting was that, under Mrs Taty's management, the girls only performed at special events held in public places such as cafés or clubs. They refused to perform at private parties and strictly adhered to the policy of only going topless.

'People assume that just because we dance topless in public, we are happy to go into a private room. No way. We dance to entertain, and sex has nothing to do with it,' Rima confirmed. She'd had to make her point because strippers in karaoke rooms usually offer extra services as well. They don't always offer sex but sometimes they are quite generous with their foreplay, such as giving a hand job or oral sex. And most of the time the foreplay leads to them ending up in bed.

For one show Rima and her gang are paid between Rp500,000 (US$60) and Rp1 million (US$120) per person. And for performing at the Erotic Nurses Party, Rima and her friends were paid Rp750,000 (US$90) per person. Not too expensive, are they?

'But sometimes it depends on the deal with Mama. During peak season we can get more than Rp1 million (US$120) per show per person,' said Rima. She also told me that being a topless dancer was her profession, at least for the moment. And because of her choice of profession, some bad comments and rumours upset her. But she said she was getting used to it and accepted that it was part of her job.

'Now I don't really give a damn what people say or what they think of me,' she said lightly. But then she immediately added that she refused to be associated with call girls and hookers. In her opinion what she and her gang offered clients was totally different to being a hooker.

'We only dance on the stage, not on the bed, ha ha. If I wanted to be a hooker I wouldn't be working my ass off dancing in front of all those people. Besides, I make enough money from dancing,' Rima confirmed firmly while smoking her cigarette.

The rates for female dancers and male dancers are almost similar. A male dancer also gets around Rp500,000 (US$60) to Rp1 million (US$120) per show per person. That rate also applies to the male dancers who regularly perform at TPK Café, Sudirman, or couple dancers at ST Discotheque in Kota.

The Take-Half-Your-Clothes-Off Party

A private party was held in a private residence. Guests were not allowed to bring a date, and the policy to take half your clothes off had to be strictly obeyed. Whether it was your bottom half or your top half, it was your call.

It was such a lovely Sunday afternoon and I'd just woken up from my nap. I headed to my terrace and treated myself to a nice cup of warm tea as I relaxed. I immediately erased the idea of hanging out at the mall that Sunday afternoon because I knew it would be too crowded. Even to find a parking space I would need all the luck in the world—or a fairy godmother. I decided what I really needed was a rest, especially after the night before, hanging out with my friends in some of the coolest cafés-cum-discotheques in Jakarta.

As I sipped my tea I suddenly noticed a red invitation, wrapped in plastic, lying on the table. It was still unopened. At first I thought it was just another party invitation from some café or discotheque. But when I finally read it I realised that it was from Bondan, a friend of mine who often threw private parties. He must be planning something big, I thought. He's never used invitations like this before. It turned out I was right because printed on the invitation were silhouettes of a naked man and a naked woman. It was a very tempting invitation. It read:

INVITATION FOR PRIVATE PARTY
TAKE-HALF-YOUR-CLOTHES-OFF PARTY
Hi guys,

Just pick: bottom half off or top half off?
Come alone and find ur other half here!
Saturday, 24th May 2003
9 pm till you drop
Jl. KTD No 9xx, Kemang, Jakarta Selatan

This was some invitation indeed. It was definitely going to be a very exclusive private party. I had to attend. Bondan is a very wealthy thirty-three year old who owns two restaurants and a yacht-rental business. This was the third half-naked party he'd organised. As I recall he threw similar parties in 2001 and 2002.

The party was to celebrate the ninth anniversary of one of his businesses as well as his thirty-fourth birthday. I know him well enough to say that this bachelor—who, despite not getting any younger, still thinks it unnecessary to tie the knot—still makes celebrating his birthday with a crazy, unforgettable party his top priority.

'It is just a question of choice. I easily get bored with conventional parties: get drunk, trip, hire a stripper ... humph, so boring. I want something different, something big,' said Bondan with his usual confidence. At that time I'd known him for about two years. He's quite famous in some exclusive nightclubs in Jakarta, especially karaoke clubs because he feels they are more private. They make great places for him to date his ladies. Bondan prefers to just have fun with his women, no strings attached. Sometimes he just goes clubbing at a discotheque, but he's never been interested in cafés, even though he lives near to some of the hottest cafés in Kemang.

'I'll go to a café if it's a really cool special occasion,' he told me.

It was becoming a habit for both of us to meet up. At least once a month we would go to a music lounge, or hang out at some mall for afternoon tea and talk about the latest hot gossip in Jakarta's world of love sprees.

The Topless Party

I wouldn't have missed this party for the world. The following Saturday, D-Day, I headed to Kemang at around 9 pm. Kemang is famous for its cafés and for being a residential area popular with expatriates. There is always something happening there, especially at weekends.

Finding Bondan's house was not hard, even though it is tucked away behind a main road. I just drove straight up Kemang Road and turned left not far from DB Café. A short distance from there I found a group of huge houses, and after turning twice more I found Bondan's house. As I knocked on his front door I remembered other parties that he'd thrown in the same house.

When I went inside I saw men and women, some good friends of Bondan, others friends of friends. Everyone was single. And, just like at previous parties, the guest room had been transformed into a huge ballroom where men and women could mingle. But before anyone could be let into the party they first had to show their invitation and sign the guest book. Two beautiful ladies stood at the door to assist the guests.

After signing in, each guest then had to choose which half of their clothes they wanted to take off, top or bottom. The two girls on the door then put the guest's clothes inside a locker and he or she was allowed in.

'Oh my god, you came too!' Sisca exclaimed when she saw me. She gave me a warm smile. Sisca is the girl who I occasionally meet at her usual hangouts: cafés in Jakarta which are popular with expatriates, such as JC in Senayan, BT or KT near Sudirman. She'd come to Bondan's party with with two female friends.

Sisca is well known for both her jobs. The first is her official job as a sales promotion girl (SPG), while her second job, her job on the side, is as a hooker. She must be pretty good at her second job because she is in the 'Ivy League', commanding payments of over Rp5 million (US$600) per date. Her ammunition is her tall and slender figure, fair smooth skin and pretty face. She uses her official job as an SPG to meet high-profile clients.

Looking around I saw that some of the guests were still outside on the terrace, while others had already gone inside. I realised that Sisca was not the only person there that I knew. I saw a few other familiar faces, people I see on my nights out.

'Aha, just because it says private party you show up alone.' My friend Jody punched me lightly on my shoulder.

'So you're here too. I thought you would be busy with your boyfriend.

Where is he?'

'Are you nuts? He's around ... somewhere. But tonight it's time for me to have a lil' fun,' he said coquettishly.

I shook my head and smiled. Jody is gay and I have known him for a year. Sometimes I run into him hanging around the mall, and on Saturday nights I occasionally bump into him at HI Discotheque near Ancol. The discotheque regularly holds gay nights.

I left Jody and carried on checking out the party. What I saw was odd, sensuous and intriguing. The guest room was about twice the size of a volleyball court. Lots of half-naked men and women had gathered there. Some of them had their tops on with their bottom halves exposed (their private parts were still covered). Others had kept their bottoms on and were exposing their top halves to the chilling air-con.

Just as with a café or a club, there was also a mini-bar with waitresses serving guests. A DJ was filling the room with energy by playing upbeat music, even though the sound system was not as loud as that of a real nightclub. The party was overflowing with alcohol—and it was free, too. Waitresses, most of them topless, were making their way around the room serving different kinds of alcohol. Near to the bar there was a long table covered with delicacies. To make the party even livelier there was a sexy couples dance performance. Three guys and three women were dancing sultrily, becoming one as the beat of the music guided them. No wonder the party was heating up. The alcohol was driving both the men and the women, and the music was making people completely wild. There was no cake, no candles, no singing 'Happy Birthday' as you do at a traditional birthday party.

Bondan, who'd chosen to expose his upper body, was busy mingling with his guests. The people he'd invited were a mixture of business clients, business partners and friends he just hangs out with. The people he didn't know were friends of friends.

This was the third time I was in the middle of a group of people who were having the time of their lives. Those who'd managed to find their 'match' at the party were now keeping each other busy. That made it harder for those who were still 'single' as it meant they had to hunt harder to find their mate. That was the reason why Bondan had not allowed couples: the party itself was the place where you were supposed to meet your partner for the night. The only thing was that at Bondan's party there were no rooms provided where you could get fast love. As you know, many clubs such as CG—the one-stop entertainment hub at Mangga Dua, Jakarta Barat—have huge karaoke rooms where the action usually takes place. Some massage parlours provide rooms with a bed, air-con, shower, TV and towels. Bondan's half-naked party was supposed to be more the rendezvous point where couples could meet. They then had to take their love adventure somewhere else.

'If they want to get laid, it's their business, not mine. I just hope they remember to pay the hotel bill. My house is just the meeting point, nothing more. I am not a pimp, duh!' Bondan laughed.

From 9 pm till after midnight the party was a blast. Around fifty to sixty people were mingling, dancing and laughing inside the guest room. And when guests had to dance together there was no shyness or awkwardness between them.

'The people who come to my party know the rules and they prepare themselves for it. If they aren't prepared, they won't come in the first place. Luckily my friends are used to this so no problem,' said Bondan while sipping his Martel. But Bondan admitted that when he threw his first half-naked party some of the guests were shy. But as the night went on, alcohol took over and more and more people started mingling with each other. They slowly got used to the idea.

'Besides,' he said, 'some of the guests are quite used to our nightlife, so a party like this is no longer a surprise. The more they get used to it, the easier it is for them to take their clothes off.'

When dawn broke some of the guests who had found their dates took off to finish the adventure. Others stayed and kept on dancing and drinking.

'It's pretty obvious that anyone who has found his or her partner will probably leave the party sometime after 2 am. But if anyone wants to stay then they are welcome to,' Bondan explained.

A take-half-your-clothes-off party is also known as a topless party. For some guests it is just the first step before moving on to a crazier party, such a nude party. Some of the guys at Bondan's I'd even met before at sex parties.

'That is Jay, my business partner.' Bondan pointed to a guy not far from where we were standing.

'I think I know that guy. We've met before at a nudies party,' I said. After we'd been properly introduced, Jay and I chatted. Bondan was a good host, introducing his guests to each other. He also introduced me to some of his female friends. There was dark-skinned Ruri who had a killer body and she was quite tall. There was Cory, a twenty-four-year-old girl with fair skin and a short haircut. Not forgetting Ami, Rosi, Nona and many more.

It was not surprising that Bondan's girlfriends were mostly easy-going and straightforward. There was no shyness. Even if the conversation was becoming too flirtatious, hinting at a one-night stand, the girls took it light-heartedly. Maybe it was because the evening was in full swing and alcohol had started to take control. Cory had already done eight tequila shots and drunk five small B52s (a mixture of Baileys, Kahlua and Cointreau, usually served in a small shot glass). Her face began to turn red and she was speaking more confidently too.

Having a one-night stand after the party was becoming an important part of the agenda for most of the guests. The unlucky guys who hadn't managed to find dates were forced to retreat back to karaoke rooms for the more conventional method. Back to basics! Some of the guys opted for this as it was already gone 3 am and they still hadn't found partners.

'Let's go to karaoke. Let's hire a stripper or Chinese female escort,' they said.

'You're not going home already are you, guys?' Bondan giggled.

The party was cooling down and the night was getting more mellow. Slow songs, like 'I'll Make Love To You' by Boyz II Men, started playing. Life was not always fair. Some had found their one-night stands at Bondan's party, while others had to go further out into the night for a second round of hunting.

Trophy Guys—
The Arisan Sex Club

Arisan is a social gathering attended by groups of women to help strengthen social bonding. The events take place in private residences, or in cafés or restaurants. The women gather to talk, mingle, eat and drink. Usually at the end of the event, each woman puts some money or goods into a pot. This is considered the prize. A winner is then randomly selected and she gets to take the prize money home. In the case of one arisan club, however, it wasn't money they were after but a guy they'd hired for the evening as their 'trophy'.

At this particular arisan club meeting, the crowd was full of joy. It was like a big party where everybody was having a great time. There was laughter and cheering from every corner, and even though there was no music you could still feel shivers run down your spine. In one corner of the room ladies were trying on new shoes, jewellery and bags. This was not a women's bazaar, but a meeting of one of the arisan clubs which have become popular in Jakarta.

Arisan used to be an old-fashioned custom among ladies in *kampung*s of old but nowadays it is making a comeback. Arisan is such an interesting concept because even when the economy is doing well, some women still prefer to save their money by joining arisan. It is said that arisan first started among lower-class women as a way for them to keep their social lives going and save money at the same time. Who would have thought that today even high-society women take part in it?

The Hip Arisan Gang

There are a lot of women in Jakarta who feel that it is important to do something productive during their free time. It is well known that hanging out at the mall for afternoon tea, taking a coffee break or even harmless window shopping can make you spend money. That is what prompted a lot of gangs or groups of women to start holding arisan events in their free time. You only have to browse cafés at the malls or plazas on Fridays and Saturdays and you will find not only women who are shopping and dining there, but also small groups of women who are attending arisan clubs.

Today there are a lot of arisan gangs. Some are more popular than others because their members are high-class ladies, top executives, socialites, the housewives of high-profile husbands or even celebrities. A celebrity arisan gathering is also known as an arisan *gaul* gang. *Gaul* is Indonesian slang for a socially active and hip person. MF is one of the most popular arisan *gaul* gangs around.

The MF Arisan Group was started by ladies of leisure. Bored of spending their free time shopping in first-class boutiques or spending hours in exclusive beauty salons, they decided to start an arisan group. Today the group has over two hundred members. They are all brand-conscious and very fashionable ladies, so it is hardly surprising that every time they hold an arisan it is like a huge glamorous party.

The ladies are all from different backgrounds. Some are divorced or widowers, some are housewives and some are still single. Their professions also differ greatly: owners of boutiques and beauty salons, sellers of fine jewellery, executives and celebrities. Imagine the scene when they all gather at some café or restaurant. Before picking the winner of the prize, the women chat, tell stories and gossip. And those who own boutiques usually offer up garments from their latest collections.

Each arisan group usually has a bookie to collect the payment from each member. The amounts usually vary from Rp1 million (US$120) to Rp2.5 million (US$300). Some even go up to Rp5 million (US$600). Each payment is separated based on the needs and flexibility of the member. So the larger the contribution, the larger the prize will be. For example if someone puts in Rp5 million (US$600), their prize would be about Rp70 million (US$8,400). If someone puts in Rp2.5 million (US$300), they would take home about Rp27.5 million (US$3,300) in prize money.

The arisan event is held once a month, but these ladies also meet for other activities, such as dance classes, throwing charity events or parties, or simply shopping at the malls.

As for parties, these ladies are party-lovers. They just love the atmosphere and the spirit of the festivities. If one of the members has a birthday party, it is always a huge, glamorous event—and not to be missed. Once, one of the members secured a multi-billion-dollar project so she decided to throw a party to celebrate. It was an enormous party. The entertainment menu was complete with sexy male dancers as well as performances from famous singers. Wow! Lucky for me I was invited. Guests were dancing on top of the bar and five male dancers were dancing sultrily. For these male dancers this was nothing unusual. They knew they were only there to get the party started. They didn't worry that people would think badly about them as this is now quite normal in Jakarta.

'The dancers weren't totally naked. They still had their underpants on. Anyway, I came with my hubby so I don't think there'll be any problem,' said Flora, who is thirty-four. She is a lovely lady and also the leader and bookie of the MF Arisan Group.

The Male Trophy

Flora's gang is quite famous as an arisan *gaul* gang, but Veronica's arisan gang is another story. Veronica is thirty years old and runs a beauty salon and boutique. Once a month she teams up with other ladies for a 'special' arisan. They're all a mixture of singles, widowers and married women. Veronica's group has almost a hundred all female members and she is both the leader and the bookie. All their parties are, of course, only open to members. The only guys they invite are close relatives, such as partners, husbands or secret lovers. Luckily for me these past two years I have always been invited as their photographer, taking pictures of the events. That was why I was there that particular night.

'Don't forget to bring a lot of rolls of film because it's going to be one hell of a party,' Veronica said when she called to invite me.

Once a month Veronica and the gang throw an arisan party at some café, hotel, karaoke club or private house. The set-up is pretty much the same each time. Each member pays a fee of Rp2 million (US$240), then at the end of the party someone picks a lucky winner. But what makes Veronica's arisan different to others is that not only does the winner get to take home all the prize money, but she also gets a special bonus: a male trophy, real flesh and blood. Usually he is a gigolo or male whore who has been booked and paid for in advance. They pay him out of the fee money that has been gathered from the members, and whatever is left over also goes towards paying for the hotel room.

'I don't want it to be just an ordinary arisan where women just gather to chat, eat, drink and gossip. It's just so lame, so boring,' said Veronica.

The particular arisan I was invited to photograph took place in late February 2003. Because it was to celebrate the twenty-eighth birthday of Maya, one of the members, it was held in a karaoke room at a four-star hotel around Kuningan, Jakarta Selatan. Maya is a single businesswoman, although no one knows exactly what kind of business she does. She is well groomed, drives an expensive Mercy, wears high-end branded clothing and owns a huge house in Pondok Indah.

Rumour has it that Maya is the mistress of some successful businessman who owns companies such as petrol stations and banks. As far as Veronica's arisan gang is concerned, Maya's status is not a secret. In fact, many of the arisan members are also mistresses.

The night of Maya's birthday I arrived at the venue at about 7.30 pm. I'd been asked to take some pictures of the members before the arisan began. Although this was considered to be a 'casual' arisan, all the women had spent hours and hours at the beauty salon having their nails, hair and make-up done for the big event.

'It would be such a shame to go to all this trouble to look good and not get a picture,' said Veronica coquettishly while striking a pose next to Maya. There were at least seventy women in the VIP karaoke room, a room that had a capacity for a hundred standing. Usually the trophy male is kept hidden in another room, but this night was different. Since it was Maya's birthday, Veronica had made arrangements for three male trophies instead of one. The boys were all brought into the karaoke room and asked to dance with only skimpy underwear covering their bodies. And because it was Maya's birthday, she was automatically the winner of the arisan.

The party kicked off. All the ladies were having fun, chatting, dancing and drinking while their trophies danced sexily in the middle of the room for at least half an hour. The girls were becoming wild, and started to tease the three trophies, pinching them, stroking them fondly and even touching their private parts. The three male dancers just smiled, even though their bodies were being sexually harassed. In fact, the more the ladies cheered, the bolder the men became.

Because it was her birthday, Maya became the host of the party. She was asked to dance between the male dancers, and because she was the host she had no choice but to dance with those sweaty sexy boys. Some of the male guests who were there were also enjoying the party. To make it even more fun they were proposing toasts nonstop. After the dance was over Maya was asked to pick one of the three trophies. The crowd cheered wildly, teasing her.

'So which one do you like, dear? The one with the crew cut, or the one who looks like Nicolas Cage? Ah, they are all so cute,' said Veronica. She was sweating all over and her breath smelt of alcohol.

'I want to drink my Illusion first,' Maya replied smiling.

I don't really know who picked him, but suddenly the guy who looked like Nicolas Cage was asked to go and wait for Maya in a hotel room.

'C'mon, Maya, honey, don't keep the prince waiting too long,' teased Veronica.

I'm not sure if the guy really did look like Nicolas Cage or whether it was just another delusion brought on by too much alcohol. Everyone looks much better when you're drunk, don't they? The karaoke room was also a bit dim, so everyone looked like they could be someone famous.

'We don't care if the guy doesn't really look like Nicolas Cage. What's more important is that the party is a huge success and Maya doesn't turn down her date,' Veronica said.

The arisan that Veronica and the gang held for Maya's birthday was not technically an arisan since the money collected was used to cover expenses: the rent of the karaoke room, the gigolos and so on. So really it was more like a fee everybody had to contribute to share in the celebration of being young, rich and alive.

'You see, this is what makes our arisan different from others. Usually people who join arisan want the money. In our club we get something that money can't buy—pleasure, both physical and mental.' Veronica smiled and took a sip of her Illusion cocktail.

Threesome Striptease— Private Live Show

I once saw a live performance by three erotic striptease dancers. The male and female strippers gave a breathtaking show that was no different to a threesome scene in a triple-X-rated movie.

The nightlife in Jakarta seems to be getting hotter and hotter, not to mention more indecent and bolder. And it is not just regular nightclubs where this is taking place but private residences too—and the entertainment there is sometimes crazy and unbelievably shocking.

Why do I say that?

Well, it all began with my friend Jeffry. He's thirty-one years old, married with two sons and owns a production house and a showbiz company. One night he invited me and some other close friends to have dinner with him at his studio in Pasar Minggu, Jakarta Selatan. But what started as a dinner turned out to be an intimate private party, with a touch of entertainment to make it more interesting.

The dinner officially started at 7.30 pm and was complete with alcohol. For the occasion Jeffrey had hired two bartenders to serve us special drinks. Bartenders are always a must for Jeffry, who is a heavy drinker. Sex On the Beach is his favourite cocktail. After we'd eaten we drank some alcohol, put on some music and danced around a bit. There were about eighteen people there, including myself.

Most people left at around 9.30 pm, but Jeffry invited about six of us to stay a bit longer. Later I found out that Jeffry had already made arrangements for the 'after party'. We were all really curious about this party, which he called a 'surprise party'. We tried to ask him more about what was on the menu but he just smiled.

So while we waited for his surprise, we kept on drinking and chatting, sharing stories that had been passed among our friends. Out of the other five people there, two were female. One was a twenty-seven-year-old girl called Lora, and the other was Dindy, who was twenty-five. Both were Jeffry's business partners. I knew them as well, and we sometimes hung out together.

The other three male guests were also close friends of Jeffry. I only recognised two of them, Tio and Budi. Some of the other guests who had already left had given excuses, such as the wife factor or the work factor, but some had also gone because they'd drunk too much.

'Are you guys bored?' Jeffry asked us. 'Wanna see something refreshing and spectacular? Let's go to my apartment. I guarantee it's going to be awesome and I bet you'll like it.' Jeffry was beginning to drop hints about his mysterious surprise party.

As well as his house in Tebet, where he lived with his wife and kids, he also owned an apartment which he used occasionally when he wanted to relax on his own. He said it was necessary to have his own sanctuary where he could get away from the stresses of work and daily life.

We hung on his every word, getting more and more curious about what the surprise was going to be, but still he refused to answer any of our questions. So on the way to his apartment we were all busy trying to figure out why on earth we couldn't have carried on the party at the studio.

'Just shut up, guys! No more questions, okay?' Jeffry laughed at our curiosity. Then he just smiled.

Dirty Dancing

The other five guests travelled in one car and I went with Jeffry. It was already 10.25 pm when we entered the car park of SR Apartments in Jakarta Selatan. The apartments were divided into several towers, and Jeffry lived in Tower Eight, which was located at the front, near a main road. We parked our car in one corner of the car park while the other car searched for a parking space.

'Hey, wait up guys! Wait for us in the lobby,' Lora yelled out of the car window.

Jeffry's apartment was on the fourteenth floor and painted beige. It looked opulent. From the window we could see the lights of Jakarta glowing beautifully, and the pool, which was next to a flowery garden. The living room of the apartment was quite big, with a table and chairs, a fridge, a twenty-one-inch TV and a VCD-DVD player.

While the six of us admired his apartment, Jeffry asked his two maids to prepare some snacks and drinks. Then he made a call to someone on his phone. I tried to eavesdrop on the conversation, but it was hard to hear what he was saying. However I did know that it had something to do with the surprise we were about to get. When he finished talking on his phone, Jeffry turned to us and told us that our surprise party would start soon.

'Why don't we have a drink first?' Jeffry suggested. 'Wanna get drunk? Please, help yourselves. Make yourselves at home. The surprise will begin in about twenty minutes.'

On the living room table Jeffry had placed a number of alcoholic drinks: Hennessy XO, Black Label, vodka, Jack Daniel's, Jim Beam, red and white wine and some snacks. After a while the living room turned into a small disco with dance music softly playing. Then we started talking, joking around, dancing a little bit and downing lots of alcohol.

Time flies when you're having fun. It was about 11 pm when we heard someone knocking subtly on the door. Jeffry quickly opened it and two men and two women warmly greeted him. One of the men worked for Jeffry and had been assigned to go and pick up his 'order'.

Jeffry let them in and introduced them to us. One of the girls was twenty-five and called Yanti. The other one was a twenty-two-year-old girl called Lissy, and the guy was Donny, who was twenty-eight. I quickly scanned the girls up and down. They both looked sexy. Yanti was tall with a curvy figure. She was wearing tight pants with a grey tank top. Lissy was of average height, and was wearing a miniskirt and tightly fitting red T-shirt.

They came into the living room where our little party was going on. All three smiled at us and politely asked if they could join in. Jeffry invited them to help themselves to the food, but it seemed like they were more interested in the alcohol. Yanti poured herself a gin and tonic, and Lissy, a vodka orange. Donny preferred a Black Label with coke. The arrival of these three guests was another hint at what was to come. I don't know about the others, but I was busy trying to guess what they were here for. My mind was racing; I knew the pattern. We all toasted each other a couple of times and chatted. It was easy to break the ice and we were all drinking more and becoming more relaxed and comfortable with each other before ... before what? I was still trying to guess, becoming more and more impatient. After mindless gossiping and a few more drinks, our three new guests asked Jeffry for permission to start their show.

'It's getting late, sir. Should we start now?' Donny asked. Jeffry nodded. Donny was right, it was getting late. Even though the living room felt a bit chilly, the alcohol heated us up inside. The music started to get a little bit louder.

At around 11.45 pm, Yanti and the gang vanished into the bathroom, which was in the right corner of the living room. I really was expecting it to be just another striptease performance, no different to those I usually saw in nightclubs. Still, I waited in anticipation.

'C'mon ... we don't have all night!' Lora spoke impatiently. In fact, we were all becoming impatient. Lora's face began to redden, a sure sign she'd drunk too much. Jeffry remained calm, sitting on the sofa, sipping his drink. His close friends, who were sitting next to him, were talking, trying to guess what Yanti and the gang were about to show us.

'If it turns out to be lame, I'm taking off. Go and treat myself to karaoke where I can have fun with Filipino or Thai girls,' Tio yelled.

Suddenly the lights went out, as if to silence Tio. Little lights—which had been placed in the centre of the living room—lit up the sofa. The room became dim. Suddenly Yanti appeared from the bathroom wearing only sheer black clothes. The blueish light exposed her body. It was clear that she was only wearing black panties, while her breasts were covered with see-through fabric, no bra. For me it was nothing special. I think Jeffry's friends thought so too because they didn't look too impressed. As I predicted, Yanti started her performance by doing some exotic moves, following the beat of the music. Her loose hair touched her breasts, her eyebrows looked dramatically long and her lips were painted red.

While Yanti was dancing sultrily, Lissy entered the room. She was smiling, her hair tied in a small bun which left her neck exposed. She was dressed exactly the same as Yanti. Seductively, both of them began to move together to the rhythm of the music. We were transfixed. Sometimes they shook their hips, other times they touched each other passionately. On a few occasions they swished their hair and rolled their hands together.

Jeffry was watching the girls without any sign of emotion. Even though it was such an eye-catching performance, for us it was still rather an anticlimax. No one watching seemed very enthusiastic, even when the girls began to strip.

'I watch things like this almost every week at DG Karaoke in Kota,' Tio whispered in my ear. Yanti and Lissy started to approach us but still we felt nothing. All that had changed were our faces, which had reddened from the alcohol. We knew what was coming next: usually after girls strip it is normal for them to tease customers by touching and pinching them in all the right places. Sometimes they glue themselves to the clients. And that was exactly what Yanti and Lissy did next.

Then it was time for Donny to perform. This macho guy, who was good-looking, began moving his body under the dim lights. He wore nothing but tight, black briefs to cover his private parts. Donny then joined the girls and they all began to dance sexily. It wasn't long before Yanti and Lissy had moved closer to Donny, and their bodies became entwined. Their performance then became even more vulgar because the movements they were making were no different to the action you see in a blue movie.

They had finally got our full attention. Such steamy dancing was really turning us on. For the next few minutes we watched Donny, Lissy, and Yanti perform not only a striptease but also mind-boggling scenes as a threesome. I mean, it was a live show between two girls and a guy, and they were practically turning each other on, doing things that you only usually see in blue movies. And what made it crazier was that they were doing it naked!

Then I remembered that this performance was similar to those around Patpong in Thailand. Patpong has two areas: Patpong One and Patpong Two. The smaller of the two is about two hundred metres from the main roads of Silom and Surawong. That is where all kinds of 'live shows' take place.

This live performance from Donny, Lissy and Yanti was officially a live threesome. There was no shyness or awkwardness among them. I was really shocked to see it right in front of me.

The hot explicit performance continued for another couple of minutes. It certainly raised the room temperature. It felt as if the air-con had stopped working. I soon realised that we were all speechless. Even I wasn't able to slow down my heart beat until after the show was over. When the performance ended I let out a long, deep breath.

'Oh my god! That was crazy man! So hot! It was like we were in the US or something, wasn't it? So, what's next? Go home? Ah, c'mon ...' Tio rambled on, full of emotion.

The Transaction Method

According to Jeffry the dancers he'd hired had not been easy to find. He'd booked them through a mammi called Mammi Tan. She was thirty-four years old and owned a love house at Jl. PL, near Melawai, Jakarta Selatan. Jeffry told me he often ordered from Mammi Tan when he had a special occasion. If it wasn't for himself, it was to entertain those clients who expected a sensational party.

Mammi Tan manages about thirty freelance protégés who are all available for sex dates. She also has countless strippers, both male and female, who are more than ready to give mind-blowing performances. Donny, Lissy and Yanti were Mammi Tan's protégés, and Jeffry had booked them from her.

Mammi Tan's protégés are quite famous among partygoers. Those who use her usually crave something wilder than just another striptease performance. People these days tend to be more into lesbian dancing, striptease couples and orgy dancing.

Yanti said there were about eight dancers who were reserved for private bookings. This lovely girl told me that she and her friends no longer take offers from nightclubs. She said the main reason was because most nightclubs nowadays have their own in-house strippers, so they are no longer looking for freelancers. Before becoming involved in private bookings, Yanti admitted that she had worked as a stripper for Pub

Karaoke EM in Jalan Mangga Besar, Jakarta Barat. So had Lissy. Lissy came from Indramayu, Jawa Barat. She told me that she once worked as a female escort at a karaoke bar in Pluit, Jakarta Utara. Her main responsibility had been to accompany the guests whilst they were singing, but she said that sometimes she would strip if requested. About eight months after she left her job she met Yanti, and the girls teamed up.

Since they both had experience, it wasn't very hard for them to find clients. They kept track of their customers and remained good friends with the pimps. Using that network, Yanti and the gang expanded their business. They were solid.

Yanti told me that, to make life easier, she, Lissy and two other girlfriends shared an apartment near Kemayoran, Jakarta Utara. They soon turned the apartment into a home office, since that was where they always took orders from clients who wanted to watch more than just a striptease show. They rent the place for Rp2.5 million (US$300) a year.

Their fee changes according to the request. For example, if someone wants to hire them to perform just a striptease, it only costs between Rp750,000 (US$90) and Rp1 million (US$120) per person per show. For a striptease and threesome live performance, like we saw in Jeffry's apartment, the whole package can range from Rp5 million (US$600) to Rp7 million (US$840) in Jakarta. If they perform outside Jakarta there are extra fees involved.

'The crazier the request, the more expensive it is. Besides, if they want just another striptease show, they can get it anywhere. That is why we only offer special services.' Yanti was doing a good job promoting her group.

On the night of Jeffry's party, if he'd hired three female dancers and three male dancers, rather than two girls and a guy, it would have cost him around Rp10 million (US$1,200) for one show, performed in two parts.

And what about a sex date?

Both Yanti and Lissy knew that what they were doing now would eventually lead to sex. For them, a fast love session or having sex with a client was a job on the side that they couldn't say no to. It was like a shadow that would always tag along.

'But it's better that way. Besides dancing, I can get a lot of tips if I have sex with them, so why not?' said Yanti lightly.

Swingers Party At the Casa Rosso Club

These days couples throw swingers parties where they swop partners in terms of sexual activities. Many who take part say that exchanging partners not only thrills them and turns them on, but also helps to relax them in a sensational way. Some even do it to entertain clients. Is this another indecent trend among our so-called hip urban society?

At around 3 am on a night out I usually spend an hour or two hanging out around Jalan HOS Cokroaminoto in Menteng before finally going home. It's a nice place to hang out since there are lots of hawker places there that stay open twenty-four hours. After midnight it becomes a popular hangout for people who've just finished clubbing as it's a good place to grab some late food or just wind down.

At a table in front of a *warung* (shop) called Jimmy's, Jaya, Boy and myself were talking about swingers parties, which have become quite trendy in Jakarta. Jaya, a twenty-nine-year-old lad who works for a multinational IT company in Setiabudi, was passionately sharing some new information he'd discovered about swingers parties.

'This is totally new. Are you interested in joining swingers parties on the net? It's easy as long as you stick to the rules,' he explained.

Of course that was one hell of an invitation. I mean, exchanging partners—the idea was already a big temptation. Jay said that first you have to pay Rp220,000 (US$26) as a registration fee, then another Rp2 million (US$240) as a member fee to get in and be invited to a party. So really it is just like any other sexual transaction, but through the net. The truth is that there are plenty of other types of sexual transactions you can find there. For example, it is so easy to get a 'date' with gorgeous girls who post their portfolios on the net. There are also plenty of sex sites which run their businesses through the net, and gigolos who are only after lonely ladies. These days the Internet has become a medium for sex businesses to reach out to more customers. Imagine how many people access the Internet every single day to hunt down sites they wish to see. It is an open door for the public to fulfil their fantasies. For example, if you want to date a call girl, you can first search on the net, make an arrangement, then meet to close the deal.

'But why bother joining through the Internet when you can just go directly to the place? It's easier. Besides, if it's only for a swingers party, I've already joined one,' I said while eating a plate of boiled egg noodles. Next to our table sat an intimate young couple. There were some small groups as well who were talking, joking and laughing together, their voices blending in with the sounds of the *pengamen* (street musicians).

Jaya's story about the swingers party was really tempting. But I wasn't convinced that just because he'd seen it on the net it was true. And even if it was true, the procedure would be a bit complicated and not very practical.

'Do you guys want to know more about the swingers party? I attended one myself three months ago.' I tried to convince Jaya.

'Seriously? Hey, you always have fun alone. Why don't you ever ask us to join in?' Jaya demanded. My other friend, Boy, who was eating a plate of *torikarage* (a Japanese dish of boneless chicken, fried with flour and served with a salad) wanted to add something too.

'Take us if there's something hip going on!' he shouted.

'Blame yourself for not hanging out much and spending too much time dating your computer,' I retaliated. Everyone laughed. Once or twice we abruptly stopped chatting, usually because we'd just noticed a gorgeous girl pass by.

The Casa Rosso Club

It was early January, five days after many hotels and nightclubs had celebrated New Year's Eve. I was about to be accidentally invited to a swing party. It all began with Rino's bet. Rino is a big guy who owns at least four discotheques in Jakarta. He also runs a distribution company that supplies goods to several of the supermarkets in Jabotabek, Jakarta, as well as in Bogor, Tangerang and Bekasi.

I know him through his girlfriend, Fenny, who is a middle-class model. She's posed sexily on the covers of a few hot tabloids, and I met her when I attended an advertising casting session in Bendungan Hilir, Jakarta. I met her again at a Valentine's Day celebration in 2002. She was in Zanzibar, near to Block M, and that was when she introduced me to Rino. After that first encounter, I met Rino again on several different occasions at malls or in nightclubs. I later found out that he was actually having an affair with Fenny while he was engaged to someone else. Fenny knew but said nothing. She seemed quite happy with the situation, especially since Roni took care of her, buying her nice clothes and make-up, giving her a place to stay and showering her with a generous allowance. For her, status was not important as long as her basic needs were fulfilled.

On the day of the swingers party I met Rino at Pondok Indah Mall. For the meeting I was told I had to bring a partner: girlfriend, mistress or whoever, as long as I was not alone. Rino made that clear. At around 4 pm I met Rino in RG Café. He'd brought Fenny. Since I didn't have a stable girlfriend at that time, I asked Yenny, one of the 'sashimi girls' I knew, to be my date. Yenny was my safety net. I knew I couldn't take regular friends because I couldn't be sure that the party wouldn't turn ugly. That was why I chose Yenny—at least she was already in the business.

'Bro, what is going to happen at this party? Give me some clues. I am really curious,' I said after introducing Yenny to Fenny and Rino.

'It's a swingers party. We tossed the room keys to find out who would end up with Fenny and who would end up with Yenny,' Rino explained lightly. Yenny, who was sitting next to me, smiled. She inhaled on her cigarette and blew out the smoke. Fenny was laughing at Roni's words. A glass of iced cappuccino, a black coffee and a plate of sandwiches were our treats that afternoon.

A swingers party? Oh my god. I must admit that I was shocked. Rino had bet me to go to a swingers party and here I was. Luckily I'd made the right decision by bringing Yenny. Imagine if I'd brought one of the female friends I hang out with? I would have left immediately.

'So, are you ok with this?' I asked Yenny.

'Of course I am ok with it. I have sex parties with my friends almost every night. Why didn't you tell me at the beginning?' Yenny replied lightly.

At around 6.30 pm we started to leave Pondok Indah Mall. Rino and Fenny went together in Rino's black Mercy E230, while I drove my Terano which, for the past two years, has become my second home with Yenny. We drove to Jakarta Barat. Rino had promised to meet his gang there at some four-star hotel. The hotel was not very far from a shopping mall near Slipi, Tomang. Rino and his gang had already booked a penthouse suite at the hotel at a cost of Rp2.5 million (US$300) per night. They'd booked it a couple of times before as it was a good rendezvous point.

It was 7.15 pm when we arrived. From the hotel lobby we went up to the eighteenth floor and knocked on the door of the penthouse suite. A waiter opened the door for us. The living room was already crowded with five couples. They greeted us warmly, and Rino introduced us one by one. It was a bit of a surprise for me because I thought the people who went to swingers parties already knew each other quite well.

'Just think of yourself as a new member. Each time we have this kind of party we usually bring a new member to spice it up a bit, hah, hah,' Rino laughed.

'Damn you. I am not a guinea pig. Luckily I'm experienced,' I replied.

At first it was no different to any other gathering. We ate, drank and chatted casually, trying to get to know each other. There was a lot of wine and beer in the fridge, and you could drink as much as you wanted. Music was playing and the twenty-nine-inch TV in the middle of the room was broadcasting a fashion show.

By 8 pm there were already nine couples there. The penthouse, which had three rooms and a large living room, was starting to feel small. Thirty-four-year-old Ivan, who'd brought his wife, was the leader of the event. It was still very casual though, and there was a light party mood. Ivan produced nine keys, put the keys inside a box and closed the lid. He had already made a list of who was going to go where. That night the guys were the ones assigned a specific room each and the ladies got to pick the keys. I was given one of the rooms in the penthouse, Rino got a room on the seventeenth floor, while Ivan was assigned the master bedroom of the penthouse. So three guys, including me, ended up in the rooms of the penthouse, while the other six guys were given rooms on the seventeenth floor.

Then it was time to choose the keys. The electric keys had already been programmed with a room number. Each lady had to pick one from the box, and the women lined up, giggling. Fenny picked a key and found out that her partner for the evening was Ivan. The girls laughed and cheered.

'Careful, don't let yourself fall under Ivan's spell. His spell comes from Japan,' teased some of the girls.

When it was the turn of Ivan's thirty-year-old wife, Paula, she slowly put her hand inside the box. She looked calm rather than anxious. When she picked the key 1802, she laughed loudly: Paula would be my partner for the night. When Ivan found out I was the one who would be spending the night with his wife, he congratulated me, tapping me on my shoulder. I didn't really understand why. When Paula realised I was to be her partner, she hugged me warmly. Then we all laughed. Unfortunately Yenny was partnered with a chubby guy name Romi, so she wasn't really laughing.

Rino got to be with his long-time partner, Yosi. She was twenty-eight years old, and they'd both been paired up at the same party three months before. That time it had been held at a villa in Puncak.

'We're reunited again, Yosi! Ah, Yosi, Yosi,' Rino kissed Yosi lightly on the check.

After the keys had all been chosen and everyone had paired off, everyone went back to dancing, drinking and chatting. At around 9 pm the couples were asked to go to their designated rooms. The swingers party had officially begun.

The next morning the couples gathered in the penthouse living room to have breakfast and morning coffee. Nothing had changed: Rino greeted Fenny, even though she'd spent the whole night with Ivan; and Ivan greeted his wife, Paula, with a kiss, even though she'd been with me the whole night.

We talked a lot during breakfast, which is when I found out that they'd been doing this for almost a year already. So far about twenty couples had joined in. There wasn't a membership fee and the procedure was quite simple. Whenever they held a party like this, each member would pay around Rp3 million (US$360). The money collected would be used to cover all expenses, including renting the penthouse, buying food and beverages. The members would take turns to be in charge every time they threw a party.

'Before you go home, don't forget to pay me Rp3 million (US$360). I paid your fee for you,' Rino told me with a grin.

'Damn. I thought it was a treat, you know, like a free trial. I'll transfer the money to you. I don't have any cash on me,' I said.

'The party isn't subsidised, you see,' explained Rino.

A while later a club named Casa Rosso held another party. That wasn't its official name, but it managed to distinguish itself from all the other sex clubs. Rumour has it that there are a lot of similar clubs in Jakarta, and Casa Rosso is only one of them.

Rino told me that the name itself had been taken from the Theatre Casa Rosso, the first and oldest erotic theatre in the world in OZ. Achterburgwal, 106-108, Amsterdam. Every night the theatre would put on stunningly choreographed erotic shows, seven days a week, nonstop. The theatre was also known for its glamorous facilities. Each of its rooms had a huge balcony, a bar and much more. Front-row guests were usually invited on stage to dance with the dancers. The dancing was marvellous, not to mention the amazing choreography, especially the love-making scenes. Such erotic and sensual scenes were common at Theatre Casa Rosso. It was just as common for Rino and his gang to host swingers parties, indulging in swapping partners for sexual pleasure.

For Paula, exchanging partners allowed her to be more open with her husband in many ways. And she was adamant that swinging was not some kind of sexual illness.

'If the husband is happy, so is the wife. So what's wrong with that? It's better to go to swingers parties together than have a man who seems happy at home but is secretly paying for whores,' Paula argued.

As for Yenny, what she did that night was a new experience. Her job as a sashimi girl enabled her to experience different things, and swinging was one of them. As for Fenny and Rino who had been members of the swingers club for almost a year, they found exchanging partners both amusing and unique. It was amusing because it happened among couples with the same mindset. And it was unique because it offered a variety of sexual thrills that were beyond the norm.

The Love House
of the Kawanua Girls

There is a small apartment occupied by beautiful girls from Kawanua. The wives and girlfriends entertain male guests, while their husbands and boyfriends gamble at the pool tables. After the girls have finished working, the couples go back to their love house.

At some of Jakarta's love-spree places that offer strippers, sashimi girls and full services on their menus, Manado girls have become quite famous. They are also known as Kawanua girls, and are in demand the most. Even at some exclusive high-end places, where members are top executives, rich college boys and businessmen, Kawanua girls are the most popular. This is true of KB Karaoke around Sudirman, MM Karaoke around Tomang, SS Karaoke around Hayam Wuruk, SD Discotheque at Kota and CG Karaoke around Mangga Dua. Kawanua girls dominate the striptease scene among these clubs. Almost ninety per cent of the girls there are Kawanua girls.

'The Kawanua girls are very warm and friendly,' said Micky, one of my clubbing mates for the past two years.

When we visited the bar where the girls worked, it was a bit dark but we could still see there were about twenty girls just waiting to be your best companion. Unlike other places, where there is a wide variety of girls, the girls here all looked quite similar. They were around 160 cm tall and in their twenties and thirties. They all had fair skin and were very fashionable. Some wore lovely nightgowns, while others were dressed in stylish jeans or miniskirts. Judging by the way they looked and talked, it seemed like they were all high school graduates. Twelve of the girls in the karaoke bar came from Manado, and they were managed by a mammi also from Manado.

'The girls in the group are not always from Manado. Sometimes we also have Javanese girls, Sundanese girls or girls from Borneo and Sumatra. But the girls here are mostly from Manado because someone brought them here to me, or other girls from Manado brought them. So actually it's a coincidence that most of them are from Manado. I can't resist them. It's very hard to find a job nowadays,' said Mammi Jessy, who was forty years old and was a Manado–Java mix. She used to be a karaoke girl herself.

Working as a karaoke girl looks so easy. You just have to have a pretty face, well-applied make-up and be easy going, especially with men. A good voice or the ability to sing isn't really necessary because your main role is to entertain the guests and keep them company. For example, Rita and Joice, two girls who accompanied me in one of the rooms, were very bold when they tried to sing some Seventies hits like 'Killing Me Softly' and 'My Way'.

But apart from that, the video with rolling text is just a standard fixture. I was told that each room there was about fifteen metres squared, with air-con, a soundproof wall and attached bathroom. However, what is much more important is the interaction between the guests and the ladies. Sometimes they just drink and talk for hours while singing and stuffing themselves with snacks. Other times some of the guests prefer to get drunk. And most of the time what happens is what usually happens between a man and a woman when they are alone in a private room.

Rita and Joice's Stories

Frankly speaking I am always interested in people's personal stories. I was curious about Rita and Joice, about their guests and, of course, about the possibility of taking the conversation to the next level.

'Are you going to take me to the Hyatt? Or, even better, to Singapore?' asked Rita playfully. Rita was a twenty-six-year-old girl from Bolang Mangandouw. After she graduated from high school she flew to Jakarta to be with her friends and relatives. 'I didn't want to stay there, stuck being a shopkeeper for the rest of my life,' she said.

She took a short course in English and secretarial studies but quit the course after less than two years and started working as a karaoke girl. Many of her friends from her home town loved to go clubbing and some of them were working as hostesses. Joice's path had been more direct. The twenty-four-year-old girl had become a karaoke girl because her senior had introduced her to it. Maybe it is because a nightlife lifestyle is more common for people in Manado.

Everybody knows that nightlife can be sinful. Rita and Joice told me they understand that the men who hire them are not just looking for companionship but also sex. Like other karaoke girls, they are more than ready to deal with the fact, even though sometimes the story varies. Rita, for example, only takes guests who she likes, while Joice only chooses ones she already knows, or who are friends of a friend. 'But with you it's okay. Your friends are bona fide, right Mas Emka?' asked Joice. Bona fide is just another word for 'big cash'. Neither of them are looking for love so there is no way they will pick someone who has no money and simply do it for love. 'I've had enough of love. I've been fooled too many times,' said Rita bitterly.

Another surprising fact is that both of them are married. Rita said she is married to Jefry, a man from Manado who is the same age as her. He used to be a musician but now he is unemployed and a good-for-nothing. Joice lives with Raymond, a guy from Maluku who works as a bodyguard around Kota. 'Don't worry, our men are very understanding,' they both said. I took that to mean that their husbands know full well that their wives work with different kinds of men and that sometimes they end up in bed with these men. 'It's very common among these kind of ladies, especially the ones from Manado,' said Micky. Then he mentioned a rented place known as Kawanua Place around Jl. Gajah Mada, Jakarta Barat, not far from the shophouses selling electronics.

Love House

Rita and Joice told me they live in the same building, like something out of the hit TV series *Melrose Place*. The rented apartment is located at Jl.

Kt, around BM, Jakarta Barat. It is a four-storey building behind an office complex, near the residential area. The first floor is used as a car park, while the other three floors contain thirty rooms, each with an attached bathroom, a living room and a bedroom. Maybe it is a coincidence, but almost eighty per cent of the people who live there come from Sulawesi Utara. The women there are famous for their beauty.

'I live here because the friends I came with lived here too,' said Joice. She told me that she lives in room 208. Rita, who had previously lived at Kalimalang Bekasi, now chooses to live in room 305 for practical reasons, such as to be more independent, to not be a burden on her relatives and the place is quite near to where she worked. Nobody really cares what she does for a living.

The other tenants, I was told, are a mixture. Some have office jobs but most of them are nightclub workers, strippers, hostesses or mammies. And just like Rita and Joice, most of them live with their spouse or partner. Rita, who had been married to Jefry for two years, said she loves the guy because he is so nice and such a good friend when she is down. Joice, who lives with Raymond, said that at the beginning he was so generous, giving her lifts to and from her work place. 'Since a lot of people here are living with their partners, I let Raymond stay here too. It's better than living alone,' said Joice.

The girls told me that Mammi Jessy provides transportation for her girls but not everybody can benefit from it because they all work different shifts. The girls who work as nightclub hostesses usually take off at around 8 pm or 9 pm, while the ones who work as karaoke girls are divided into afternoon shifts from 1 pm or 5 pm. The ones who work as strippers usually work from 6 pm to 3 am, but those who are most in demand definitely have more flexible schedules. They can go to work or go home whenever they please.

When I met them Rita and Joice were also quite famous, but top of the list at that time was Icha, a twenty-four-year-old girl who had an oval face, long black hair and sparkling eyes. She was a freelancer, working for places such as SO Karaoke at Kota, YT Karaoke at Melawai, HI Nightclub at Jakarta Utara or in four-star hotels. Icha was often seen riding her Honda City 2000. Sometimes she asked Roy, her boyfriend who was two years younger than her, to pick her up or drive her around.

Another famous girl was Rani, a twenty-one year old who had a plum figure, fair skin and 34A breasts. In the beginning she'd worked at LI as a karaoke girl, but when clients outside of the club starting booking her services, she'd decided to keep her options open. She was even given a Daihatsu Ceria car as a present from one of her regular customers who was Taiwanese.

'We never want to get involved in other people's affairs,' said Rita. 'Whether it is her husband or not, it's none of our business. We are all working for a living and we just want to have a little bit of fun, that's all,' said Rita.

That's why I think listening to the people in the building is like watching an espisode of *Melrose Place*. Men and women live there without any rules or regulations. Something that did surprise me was that the men are usually unemployed or between jobs. They spend most of their time relaxing or taking their girls to work then picking them up when it was time. While the men wait for the girls to finish their jobs, they play pool or gamble. Some even start to act like they manage their girlfriends, trying to run their schedules.

'Sometimes it really gets on my nerves,' Rita told me. 'I work hard to earn the money then he just wastes it gambling. But what can I do? I don't want to be alone.'

When they aren't working Rita, Joice and the other couples relax. They go to billiard houses to play pool or just to chill out there and listen to the music. 'It feels so different. No rush and no pressure, for sure.'

Five Million Rupiah and Above

Because of their lifestyles, living as a normal husband and wife is just not possible for the couples. Living in the 'Melrose' building costs each girl more than Rp5 million (US$600) per month: Rp1.2 (US$144) to Rp1.5 million (US$180) for the rent; Rp1 million (US$120) to Rp2 million (US$240) for food and cigarettes; Rp1 million (US$120) to Rp2 million (US$240) to buy clothes and cosmetics and pay the phone bill; and Rp1 million (US$120) to Rp2 million (US$240) to give to their spouse. The cost is higher if they are both into drugs or gambling. It is a never-ending cycle. The girls keep lighting up Jakarta's nightlife with their presence, especially in high-end places.

The meeting with Joice and Rita took place in the lobby of one of the four-star hotels in Jakarta Pusat. They'd asked for some time off to meet me, and Raymond had driven them to the hotel in Mammi Jessy's car. 'But we told him not to pick us up because you are going to drop us off, right?' she asked me.

I nodded. Joice then asked me about the room she thought I had booked for us all, but I took them to a coffee shop instead. While we all drank coffee, wine and beer, I asked them to tell me about themselves. I hoped they had stories that might be interesting and seem glamorous, full of tragedy and mystery. And I was right. It seems that behind the light-hearted nature of the shows that attract men every night there is a hidden picture of a very different life. The ladies work very hard to pay for a life they've always dreamt about, while their men suck them dry like parasites. What do they contribute?

'I'm confused. I don't want to talk about it. Just let it flow.' Rita and Joice gave up. That night they were both too tired to think about the life they were living and where they were heading. Come what may, come what may, life would flow just like the wind would always blow. They would think about a better future another time, in another life. Maybe tonight or maybe some other day ...

Gay Night and Lesbian Society

The gay and lesbian community is becoming more transparent. Gay marriages even take place in public. Do you want to know about the gay and lesbian communities in Indonesia, especially in big cities like Jakarta, Surabaya and Bandung?

'*My name is Ardiansyah. I was born in Kebumen, Central Java and I am twenty years old. Now I live in Bandung in one of my relative's houses. None of my family know my true identity. I am gay. I am very closed about the subject. I am not ready to come out. I can still control my behaviour, everything is still normal. That is why when my parents decided to set me up with some girl I just said yes. But the truth is I am more attracted to men than to women ...*

'*... once, I had a boyfriend. But sadly he broke his commitment to me. I was so heartbroken because I'm always serious in every relationship I have. I first felt I was gay when I was at junior high school. I was always dreaming about the boys I fancied. In 1998 I was a Trendy Boy Finalist, and in 1999 I was one of the finalists of Top Model Casual in Yogyakarta. That is why I am very interested in acting now ...*'

The above is an extract from Ardiansyah's confession in *GAYa Nusantara*, Surabaya, 2003 edition. Ardiansyah was on the cover of the magazine. Without any hesitation, he started telling me stories about his secret life as a gay man, hoping to find more people in his situation.

In the article there were a lot of personal stories from gays. One of them was a confession from a teenager called Sofian. Born on 3rd May

1977 in Palembang, Sofian's face was on the cover of the September 2002 edition of *GAYa Nusantara*.

'*My gay life started when I was in my last year of high school. Until now, my parents still haven't found out about me being gay. Only my close friends know. If my parents find out they will be furious and ashamed of me. If that happens, I will bear all the consequences, no matter what. I've never had a boyfriend though. My ideal guy would be masculine, nice, caring and loyal. I hate people who cheat. If my future boyfriend was to have an affair, I would either have confront him or I would cheat myself ...*'

In that same edition was a confession by Aria. He was twenty-three years old and came from Bukit Tinggi, West Sumatera. He told many stories about his experiences:

'*I was born into a very humble family. When I was seven, my dad fell ill and six months later he died. My mother then had the responsibility of feeding the entire family. We were eight children, all very young. My mother had to sell our house and our land to pay our debts.*

'*I started to like boys when I was in junior high school. My first crush was on a guy who was my class leader. I kept his name in my heart. I didn't want anybody to know that I was gay. After I graduated from junior high, I didn't go to senior school because we were too poor. We had no money for my education so I went to Medan to look for a job. After a while I got to know where my kind usually gathered, and that was where I had my first gay relationship. It was with a doctor.*

'*I started a relationship with a guy named Mas Agus. He was so mature which I liked. For me Mas Agus was like a father, a mother, a brother, a teacher and also a lover. Our relationship lasted for two years until one day I caught him having affair with my friend Dion. So we split up and I started a new relationship with Andre. I dated him for one year until, for reasons still unknown to me, he dumped me. Right in front of my eyes he began dating much older guys. I was heartbroken. That was why I left Medan and headed to Surabaya.*

'*It was really hard living in Surabaya. I couldn't find a job. One night I was standing near Tugu Pahlawan (Pahlawan's Monument) when suddenly a car stopped in front of me and a middle-aged man started coming towards me. He introduced himself as Om Benny (Uncle Benny). That very night Om Benny took me to a hotel near Darmo. Since then I've been living my life as some guy's pet or 'cat'. I don't want to live this way, but I have no choice. Now I am twenty-three years old and I want to continue my education. I want to get a degree, but is it possible?'*

Everyone's path through life is different, just as everyone's sexual orientation is different. There are some guys who prefer guys to women, some guys who prefer other women instead of guys, and some who are in between.

Homosexuals in Indonesia are not like useless pieces of paper that fade when the wind blows or vanish when it starts to rain. Each day the gay community is getting bolder and bolder, showing their true identities in public areas. Years ago these couples would have remained silent. Gays in Indonesia have their own ways of expressing themselves. One is through the aforementioned magazine, even though there are limited copies and it is strictly for gays only. At least they have something through which to express themselves. The confessions of Ardiansyah and Sofian are just two examples of gays who have dared to publicly speak up. There are a lot more like them in Indonesia.

In March 2003 I was very glad to be invited to the offices of *GAYa Nusantara* in Surabaya. For several days I was able to talk to the gay community and to GN's activists. They revealed a lot to me about their daily lives. I found them very chatty and good to talk to about any subject. I also found the same thing when I visited Malang and met with IGAMA (a gay community in Malang), and IWAMA (a transvestite association in Malang). We even did *ngeber* (field research) at Tugu Station where transvestite hookers usually operate.

It was 10 pm and the cool weather of Malang was starting to chill my spine. I was sitting in a coffee shop next to the station. With me were Ipul, IGAMA's chief, Merlin, IWAMA's leader, and Mister Dede Oetomo, a counsellor with GN. We sipped hot coffee and ate snacks of fried tofu and tempe. Some of the transvestites who were nearby dropped in to join us.

'There aren't many people about tonight, Sister Merlin. There is a football match on,' said Waty, who was wearing a miniskirt and baby-blue tank top. Waty was, of course, not his real name.

Waty was flirtatious and explained what was a typical night for him. He said that usually he could get between five and seven male clients per night. If there weren't many clients around, like that night, he would usually get only three customers. Waty said that after being with a lot of men he'd seen his fair share of bizarre behaviour. Like the time when a big macho guy hired him and brought ladies' clothes. Before the sexual transaction took place, he changed into the outfit.

'I guess he likes to be a woman during sex. Since he paid me a lot of money, I didn't mind,' said Waty, giggling as he remembered the story. That night he had had just two clients.

Ipul and Merlin did this *ngeber* once a week. The aim was to give the transvestites counselling and raise awareness about the dangers of HIV and AIDS.

'That's why every chance we get, we tell them to wear a condom for every single sexual transaction they make,' explained Merlin, who had been in the movement for quite some time. He often met with other transvestites in Malang for health education purposes. Anyone who didn't know him well enough would easily mistake him for a woman. Merlin had a slender figure, a pretty face and medium-length hair. He wore a miniskirt and a tight-fitting top. He even wore make-up. His lipstick made him even more gorgeous.

Out of curiosity I asked Merlin why a lot of men still paid for sex with a transvestite, even though they knew the transvestite was actually a man.

'Who knows a man's secret better than another man? That's the key,' he said. Hmm, that makes sense. 'That's why once a man has had sex with a transvestite he will keep going back for more,' Merlin giggled.

We stopped the counselling session at 1 am. From my conversation with Mister Dede Oetomo, Merlin and Ipuy, I had managed to obtain a lot of information about the gay scene. I discovered that there were many reasons why a man could be gay. Firstly there is the gene factor, where a man's female hormones develop faster than the male hormones. There is the influence of his family, where the boy copies the behaviour of his dominant female siblings. But the most common factor is that of his environment. For example, if a guy spends most of his time playing with female friends, then subconsciously he starts to copy their behaviour and that is when he turns gay. In the most common scenario he spends so much time with male gay friends that he considers being gay a new trend. In some cases a man hates women because he has his heart broken in a bad relationship. That is when he turns gay.

Aside from the aforementioned, there are some men who turn gay due to economic pressures. They are forced to sell their bodies to other men to make money.

Jakarta's Nightlife

The development of the gay community in Indonesia is so dynamic. More and more gays are starting to publicly come out, and some are even struggling to be acknowledged. Certain clubs in Jakarta have become their favourite hangouts. One of them is Jalan-Jalan Café on the thirty-sixth floor of Menara Imperium (Imperium Tower). On Sunday night laughter fills every corner, blending with the music. You can hear some of the words transvestites like to use: *sutra* meaning 'enough', *roxena* for 'cigarette', *sukria* for 'like', *mabora* for 'drunk', *padang sahara* for 'very hot temperature', mascara for 'entry', *maharani jody* for 'expensive', *macarena* for 'eat', *tinta bis kota* for 'cannot' and *jelitur* for 'ugly'.

These gays usually hang out on Sunday nights. Talking in high-pitched tones they sound like women but physically they are all well-groomed men. Sometimes they highlight their hair and they love to wear tight-fitting clothes. Some of them look like average men, dressing casually. Not all of them flirt and some speak just like men.

The particular Sunday night I went to Jalan-Jalan Café it was full, unlike some nightclubs that are usually not very crowded on this day of the week. Hundreds of guests were there, most of them men and most of them gay. They all came from different backgrounds. There were designers, executives, stylists, models, choreographers and many more. I even recognised some familiar TV celebrities.

Another time when I went there the club was hosting a gay night.

115

It was a special event with cowboy dancers, and at around 11 pm four men got up on the stage. They were wearing tight black shorts to cover their private parts, and had athletic bodies. Their muscles and oily skin were glowing in the spotlight. The audience cheered and screamed wildly when the dancers started to shake their bodies. Of course, the loudest screams came from the gay men. They screamed even louder when the dancers finally approached the guests.

Jalan-Jalan Café held its first gay night back in 1997. Every year since then the demand had grown more and more. That is why every Sunday night from 9 pm to 2 am they have special gay events. Every week they have male go-go dancers, and once every two weeks they throw special events, such as a Fashion Dance Show or a Comedy and Cabaret Show with Tata Dado and The Silver Boys. Tata Dado is a famous cross-dressing actor who usually performs a comedy act and The Silver Boys are a group of transvestites he co-ordinates. Sometimes the café throws a body-builder show too. Similar events are also held at Moonlight around Kota. The discotheque is in an old colonial building not far from the big intersection at Jalan Hayam Wuruk. It is one of the coolest places for gays. It was known for years as the favourite hangout for gays in Jakarta, and almost every night there was a gay invasion.

It's common for gays there to dress up in different costumes. Some dress up in different male costumes while others put on women's clothes. The Moolight Discotheque is the place where gays and transvestites blend as one. On special nights they throw events like drama sessions, catwalk contests, celebrity look-alike contests and sexy dance performances. There they can express themselves freely from 10 pm till 2 am. Before gay cafés started to appear everywhere, Moonlight had been the pioneer.

'As long as we can be happy and hang out with our kind, that's all we want. It's very hard to be happy in Jakarta, you know,' said Dra, a twenty-four year old who worked as a stylist. Even though a lot of similar cafés are popping up, Moonlight still has its place in the hearts of gays.

Nowadays gays in Jakarta spread themselves between many different hangouts. Another café that has become a trendy gay hangout is Blue Prints Bar. It has positioned itself as a gay bar but on Mondays it holds an event called Monday Big Banana where male go-go dancers perform. The event starts at 11 pm and ends at 1 am. In mid-August 2003 I dropped by that particular café. There were a lot of gays there but not as many as there were in Moonlight or Jalan-Jalan Café.

Another popular place with gays is Hai Lai. This one-stop entertainment club at Ancol holds some events for gays. Every Sunday night it hosts events in its discotheque, restaurant, karaoke bar or sauna. The one in the discotheque makes use of the club's big stage. The scenes are not much different to those you find in the gay community. There are a lot of shows where a guy is the mascot and a group of gays dance on the dance floor or get down to some serious action on the stage.

Apart from these hangouts and clubs, the gay community in Jakarta has another venue that is unbelievably hot for them: a lovely afternoon at the swimming pool and sauna of Hotel NO around Jakarta Pusat. Not to mention the beauty salons around Tebet and Senopati, Jakarta Selatan.

Café A2 is another place where gays go at weekends, and gays who hang out in cafés are usually thought to be the most hip and trendy. The gay night at Café A2 is held every Wednesday, breaking the unwritten rule that every Wednesday night has to be Ladies Night.

I almost forgot to tell you that gay clubbers never miss the opportunity to dress up every time they go out. They always look so trendy and unique. Among Jakarta's gay clubbers there are some familiar faces. For example JR, a hot young actor who has starred in many television dramas and is now a big teen star. Then there is GI, a young fashion designer who has now embarked on an acting career. Not to mention RA, MP and AG who are the most famous male models in Jakarta.

For them, clubbing is a way to socialise and meet new people.

'I come here with my friends to break the monotony and hopefully get myself a new boyfriend,' said Stan, a twenty-three-year-old gay who is the assistant of a famous pop singer. According to Stan looking for a new date in the club is not easy, especially if you are a new kid and nobody knows you. You have to really understand the subtle signs of the other gays as some have their own moves when it comes to getting a date. Some will take a 'closer' look at you in the bathroom, carefully watching your every move and paying attention to every little detail of the outfit you are wearing because some gays identify with a certain earring or type of clothing. But a gay clubber like Stan wouldn't go to A2 to find a partner—you go to Moonlight for that. For Stan just being at A2 gives him a certain sense of pride since it is a high-end club and many of the guests there are wealthy.

'Just because I'm gay doesn't mean I can't go clubbing wherever I like. I don't really care about someone else's sexual orientation, and I hate using it as a reason for why I can't socialise somewhere,' Stan explained. Maybe he is right. Gay people are no different to the rest of us. They don't all work as stylists, designers or some other profession related to the gay world. Sometimes they do regular jobs, such as engineer, banker, accountant, manager or architect.

I remember one conversation I had with Mister Dede Oetomo. He mentioned some famous names in certain governmental departments. Right from the beginning Mister Dede Oetomo never denied that he himself was gay. Everywhere and anywhere he would speak the truth. 'I don't see the point in telling lies. That's the truth. When people love each other, they shouldn't hide it,' he said in a strong East Javanese accent.

Gay people in Jakarta, just like regular people, have their own organisations. In Surabaya there is GAYa Nusantara (GN) which struggles for gay rights, holds a lot of seminars warning about the dangers of HIV and AIDS, goes straight to prostitution spots to educate gays, holds entertainment events that promote awareness about HIV and AIDS, organises seminars about gays and publishes its own magazine which gives an insight into the gay community. In Jakarta there is IPOOS, also known also as GAYa Betawi. GAYa Betawi holds similar events to GN, including entertainment shows that feature a campaign on AIDS and HIV. Every time they've had a show the crowd has been amazing and extremely supportive. It has been the same story at similar events held in Hai Lai or Moonlight on previous occasions.

GAYa Betawi is not the only gay association in Jakarta. There are others that are more private and informal, such as the one in Kalimalang. It all started when some gays and transvestites began to gather together once a month and hold arisan. They still gather and talk about their plans for organising gay events.

One of the biggest gay events I have ever encountered was held in early January 2003. For the very first time the event took place at Studio

East Discotheque. Gay and transvestite artists performed as the main act and it was open to the public. Lots of people came from all over.

The event was really big. Three transvestite divas performed: Miss Vera, Miss Paula and Miss Liza Iblis. They were amazing and seemed like really professional singers. Miss Liza Iblis was singing 'I Want To Break Free' in his/her own unique style, while Miss Paula sang Mexican songs and Miss Vera, who wore a Middle Eastern costume, shook the audience with his/her dancing. Mammi Anna led the countdown, and after that they sang the song 'Asereje'. Then Studio East started playing and people danced and laughed until morning.

In Bali the gay community is practically everywhere, in the cafés and discotheques around Kuta, Seminyak and Legian. One of the cafés popular for its gay night is Q-Bar in Seminyak. The bar is located just off the main street and every night it is full of gays, locals and foreigners.

Sekong and Hemong

By hanging out with some of my gay friends and dipping into their world I have managed to gather quite a lot of information, even down to the small details. Take the word 'homosexual', for example. For some people homosexual means gay and gay means homosexual, regardless of whether you are a man or a woman. Others have a much stricter definition and to them a man is a gay but a woman is a lesbian.

As a community, homosexual people develop their own language. The language they use is informal but it distinguishes their community and becomes their trademark. The most interesting part is to learn how the language they use first started. It first emerged by itself, then grew and changed with the latest trends. People found it so hilarious that it spread quickly and was enjoyed by many young people as *lingua franca*. Good examples are the words *sekong* and *hemong*. *Sekong* actually comes from the word *sakit*, which is Indonesian for 'sick'. *Hemong* is from the word 'homo'. As I mentioned before, at first this language in the community was like a code that outsiders couldn't understand, but then it spread and everybody was using it. How to form the language is pretty easy. You just add the suffix *–ong* to every word. For example, the word *laki,* which means 'man', becomes *lekong*. The word *asli*, which means 'original', becomes *eslong*. The word *perawan* (virgin) becomes *prewong*. *Nafsu* (libido) becomes *nafsong*, *gede* (huge) becomes *gedong*. But over time some words have deviated from their original meaning. For example, the word *dia* (she/he) has become *diana*.

Many young hip people found the language so cool and fun that they began to adopt their own vocabulary and turn it into a trendy, informal language that you use between close friends or in groups. For example, the word *sendiri* (alone) became *sendokir*, *ramai* (crowded) was substituted with *ramayana*, and *jij* (read as 'ye') comes from the Dutch word for 'you'. *Akika* replaced *aku* (I am).

Sometimes the language changes dramatically. There is no logical pattern to the words. The key to mastering the language is just to hang out a lot with the transvestite, gay and lesbian communities since they are the ones who invented and developed the language. That way you get used to the words. Below is an example of a conversation between two *binan* (transvestites) called Miki and Randy. I met them when I had a cream bath at a beauty salon around Senopati, Jakarta Selatan.

Randy: '*Jij, mawar kemandose?*'
('Where are you going?')
Miki: '*Akika mawar polonia.*'
('I want to go home.')
Randy: '*Jij, sutera makarena belanda?*'
('Have you eaten?')
Miki: '*Belanda. Ntar di rumee aja.*'
('No. I'll eat later, when I get home.')
Randy: '*Kita jail-jali dulu yuk, nek.*'
('Let's have a walk first.')
Miki: '*Mawar jail-jali kemandose?*'
('Where do you want to go?')
Randy: '*PS. Mawar belalang baju. Ikatan tinta?*'
('Plaza Senayan. I want to buy clothes. Do you want to come?')
Miki: '*Tinta. Akika janji ma lekong.*'
('No. I have a date with a guy.')
Randy: '*Ya sutra, Titi Dj ya.*'

('Okay. Be careful.')

Miki: *'Tererengkyu. Ini roxena jij. Lupita ya?'*

('Thanks. This is your cigarette. Did you forget it?')

Randy: *'Nek, adinda lekong lucita loh.'*

('There's a cute guy.')

Miki: *'Mandose? Jij, sukria sama diana?'*

('Where? Do you like him?')

Randy: *'Tuh lagi di kursi. Luncang aja. He he ...'*

('There, he's sitting on the chair. Very cute.')

Miki: *'Ah, kurcica gitu, nek. Malaysia deh.'*

('Ah, he's so thin, such a turn off.')

Most of the gays use this kind of language in their daily conversations. I often hear them talking amongst themselves in cafés, fitness centres, discotheques and so on. And as they are now bolder in public, their existence is even more obvious. Jakarta is not the only big city they live in. In some of Indonesia's other major cities, they are also starting to come out and show their true identities. Now almost every city in the country has a gay network. GAYa Nusantara (GN), Surabaya gave me the following contact details for their network in Indonesia:

- GAYa Nusantara (GN), Jl. Gubeng Kertajaya IX-B/44 Surabaya 60286
- IPOOS/GAYa Betawi, Salon Alfa Jl. Dr. Mawardi IV/21 Grogol, Jakarta Barat 11450
- GAYa Priangan, PO BOX 1819, Bandung, Jawa Barat 40018
- GAYa Siak, Jl. Kakap No. 7 Pekanbaru, Riau
- BAGASY (Batam Gay Society), PO BOX 517 BTAMSJ, Batam 29432
- GAYa Semarang, Sunarsito Jl. Ngresep Timur V/110, Semarang 5000
- Gayeng Salatiga, Shopping Centre, Ground Floor, Jl. Panglima Sudirman B1-12A Salatiga
- GUCHI (Association of Homo Guy Indonesia), PO BOX 36/YKBS, Yogyakarta 55281
- IGAMA, (Ikatan Gaya Arema), Jl. Mayjen Panjaitan

5 Malang 65145
- IGS, Indonesian Gay Society, PO BOX 36/ YKBS
Yogyakarta 55281
- IKOOS (Ikatan Orang-Orang Sehati), Salon Janis Jl.
Randu Gede Stand No. 1 Mojokerto
- GAYa Dewata, PO BOX 3769, Renon, Denpasar, Bali 80037
- GAYa Celebes-Harley Celebes, Jl. Baji Passare II
No.6 Makassar
And so the list goes on ...

The Lesbian Society

Compared to the gay community, which has really broken the mould and come out, the lesbian community is quite the opposite. In Jakarta and Surabaya, for example, lesbians are very private. Most of their activities take place among themselves. One lesbian network I discovered was Swara Srikandi, PO BOX 4966/JKP, Jakarta Pusat 10049, but apart from that it is really hard to find others. And, frankly speaking, I know some lesbians individually but not as one big community. Of those who I know, very few speak up truthfully about their homosexuality. The only lesbian who has dared to speak up was Viny, a twenty-six-year-old girl who works as an assistant manager at a café in Kemang. Viny has short hair and usually dresses in her favourite outfit: a pair of jeans and a T-shirt. She is a nice, friendly person and I have known her for almost three years. I don't see her regularly but I sometimes meet her when I'm out at night.

Three years before I met Viny she'd finally confessed that she was a lesbian. We've never talked seriously about the subject but sometimes, during our casual conversations, the subject just pops up spontaneously, such as one time when we were sitting together at some bar and I noticed there were some hunks sitting next to us.

'There's a hunk over there. Sure you don't want to make a move?' I asked curiously.

'Nope. Not my type. Haven't I told you I like girls?' said Viny.

'Are you sure?' I teased her.

'Are you nuts? For as long as you've known me, have you ever seen me with a man?' Viny was right.

A lot of nightclubs regularly throw gay nights but there are never any lesbian nights. And even if there are, the lesbians are usually very subtle about it, as if it's just another girls' night out. Sometimes they gather in small groups at HP Discotheque in Hotel AC near Matraman, or at EL Café near Block M Jakarta Selatan.

At the time of writing this I managed to log on to http://swara.cjb. net where I found a lot of information on the lesbian community in Indonesia. On the home page of the site I found some very interesting information about what the general vision and mission of Swara Srikandi is. It states that Swara Srikandi is NOT a lesbian recruitment organisation. The truth is that lesbians in Indonesia existed long before the organisation was founded. Swara Srikandi's aim is to counsel and advise lesbians on how to live among a predominantely heterosexual society in a way that can see them living a fulfilling life. It wants to put an end to the stereotyping in the media that lesbians live wild lives. It also stated that Swara Srikandi is NOT trying to increase the number of lesbians in Indonesia. If there are more lesbians in Indonesia then it is not because of the organisation.

On the website I also found an interesting article written by someone called Wina, posted on 4th October 2003 at 15:28. It was under a column entitled 'The Warna-Warni Networking Statement'. The section was for individuals or organisations that care about all subjects related to gay, lesbian, transgender and transvestite issues. These are divided into the sectors of Lesbian, Bisexual and Transgender. They include the Indonesian Women's Coalition, Jakarta and Sumatera Barat, Pelangi Kasih Nusantara Foundation, Srikandi Sejati Foundation, Swara Srikandi Indonesia, Pelangi Nusantara Yogyakarta, Qmunity and other individuals.

The following is an extract from the article:

'There are a lot of differences in everyone's lives. And with these differences we learn to see the uniqueness of every human being. Some of us appreciate and look at these differences positively. To us they provide such valuable lessons, like books that never end.

'But reality speaks differently. A lot of people in society don't really appreciate such differences. Worse, they not only deny that these differences exist, but also feel more superior and able to judge those who are different. This takes the form of violence, excommunication, condemnation, even trying to destroy the rights of others in the name of morality, religion or other terms they create to suit their goals. Those who are different are validated and victimised.'

The social reality of gays, lesbians, transgenders and transvestites

'Whether individually or as a group, we (gays, lesbians, transgenders, transvestites) have been treated unequally for a long time.

'Sick, abnormal, sinner, deviant and HIV/AIDS carrier are names they give us. In our daily lives we are often excommunicated. When we form an organisation to make ourselves feel stronger, people become suspicious and start accusing our movement of carrying out subversive acts against the government or crimes. Several times in our community, violent acts of inspection have been carried out in the name of religion or morality. One lesbian organisation in Jakarta even received several death threats because people said their blood was dirty.

'In addition the family is not very supportive, with the most hurtful comments coming from a family member. They throw us out of the house, calling us names and abusing us physically and mentally. And the country is wrong to let these awful incidents happen and not arrest those responsible.'

It's not right to force your will on others

'The unfairness of the situation emerges as the result of misunderstanding. People misunderstand the concept of heterosexuality. It is seen as the only choice for every human because it was made legitimate by religion and other social norms. Anything other than that is an illness. The truth is that society's paradigm puts heterosexuality as the absolute and universal

ideology for humans, and discussing sexuality is a big taboo. Such an absolute heterosexual paradigm does not allow for any discussion, written or verbal, about every individual's human right.

'The Human Rights Pledge clearly states that no body or group has the right to discriminate against others (individuals or groups) who are different in terms of gender, race, sexual orientation, religion, skin colour or marital status. In addition, our UUD 1945 (our Statute) strictly rules that nobody can be discriminated against for any cause, and everybody has the right to be protected from discrimination.

'So it is clear that everybody has the right to choose what's right for them without being judged, blamed or condemned for being different. Because it is everyone's right to be different, and forcing one's will onto another is in violation of that person's human rights.'

That excerpt gives an insight into the lesbian and gay community in Indonesia. Until today they are still struggling for their right to be recognised as complete human beings. They don't want to be excommunicated, excluded or marginalised. They want to be appreciated as normal human beings who can express their aspirations and rights freely—just like the rest of us.

A One-Night Stand With The Micky Mouse Girls

The girls were dressed to kill in tightly fitting mini outfits that screamed sexy. They were parading themselves around the gambling arena, preying on any lucky man who'd just made a fortune. When they found one, they would tease and seduce him with their charms before finally draining him of cash. They were The Micky Mouse Girls.

There were probably hundreds of game machines in the crowded room. They looked like children's toys except that there weren't any pictures of racing cars or animals on them. Instead each screen had a set of cards, placed in a certain order. There were seven cards, and each card represented a game. The machines were lined up in the room in an orderly fashion. People called them The Micky Mouse machines. No one knew why they were called that but these machines, on which you could play poker, were already bringing so much joy to Jakarta's night guests. A lot of men would sit religiously in front of them, trying to defeat them, their hands busy pushing buttons nonstop while they squinted carefully at the cards in front of them.

I walked around a little bit and found that there were a lot of women who wanted to try their luck too. Actually the game is pretty simple. Each player buys credit that flashes up on the machine's screen. For example, if the player buys Rp50,000 (US$6), then he gets 500 credits. Credit is called 'beat'. Then he chooses which machine he wants to play on. The cheapest one costs Rp1,000 (US$0.12) for ten beats. Or you can go for the one that costs Rp2,000 (US$0.20) per beat, or Rp5,000 (US$0.50) per beat. There are also machines that double the beat value.

Once or twice over the noise of the machine you can hear somebody yell *siki* ('straight flush' or 'royal flush') and sometimes the players splutter when they are on a losing streak. From the women who joined in the game, you can hear coquettish laughter. When the words 'straight flush' flash up on the screen, the player knows that he's picked matching cards and landed the jackpot. His prize can be anything from from Rp3 million (US$360) to Rp6 million (US$720). While the games are being played, waiters and bouncers walk around the room, watching every corner.

CT, the gambling arena at Gajah Mada, operates twenty-four hours a day, seven days a week. You can also find the same atmosphere at the CP gambling arena in Ancol, not far from a four-star hotel. At CP there are even some casinos and VIP rooms for exclusive members. Some hip Micky Mouse gambling arena called MD is located around Kelapa Gading, pretty close to a huge, lively shopping mall.

'Gambling doesn't recognise gender. Men and women can play, even though it is forbidden. As long as you have the money and the guts, just play,' said Rusli, one of my friends who works for a cargo company and likes Mickey Mouse gambling.

The Sex Area

Gambling isn't the only thing that attracts people. Many of the men who are addicted to the MM (Mickey Mouse) gambling machines are also amused by the presence of beautiful girls. And, of course, it is obvious that the girls are not there to gamble. Some might be but most of them are there to light up the nightclubs. Some of the girls shop around at nearby discotheques, some are 'singers' or 'female escorts' at karaoke clubs and some are obviously there to trade money for fast love.

The main MM gambling places are CT in Kota, CP in Ancol, RH in Mangga Dua, MO in Pasar Baru, GM in Jatinegara and MD in Kelapa Gading. All of them are located around nightclubs, be it near discotheques, clubs, karaoke clubs, hotels, massage parlours or even near apartments where high-class call girls live. That's why the later it is, the merrier the guests become.

For some call girls, MM gambling arenas are the perfect places to find a date. The reason is simple: wherever there is gambling there is also big money. And what makes it easier for the girls is the fact that most of the men who are there don't mind having a companion cosy up to them, especially after they've won millions or rupiah in one night. With between Rp500,000 (US$60) to Rp1 million (US$120) in their hands, the lucky gamblers can end up winning a 'royal flush' worth between Rp12 million (US$1,440) and Rp24 million (US$2,880).

These places are such a blessing for the girls. The old saying 'All roads lead to Rome' is certainly true; these girls have many ways to achieve their goals. They take these words to heart and are inspired to find even slicker ways to hunt down generous men who are after small pleasures. And so it has become their modus operandi to hang out in nightclubs. Whether at discotheques, pubs, karaoke clubs, hotels or massage parlours, they are everywhere almost every night. For example, there is one karaoke club where some ladies, who work as 'female escorts', are not just there to accompany and entertain the guests in the VIP room. Often they end up in bed with the guests. Some girls confess that they are officially strippers but don't mind giving the guests extra services.

So it is quite easy for the girls to operate because the MM gambling arenas are located near to where they work. Sometimes at their work places business isn't good and their client numbers are low. That can only mean one thing: less income. Less income is no good because they need to keep the home fires burning—they need to stay alive. That is when they start to look outside of their work places for other opportunities.

Going back on the streets is not an option. For those girls who are someone's mistress, the situation is quite stable since they have someone to look after them. These girls have their monthly allowances so they don't need to worry about whether they are able to eat every day. But for the girls who survive day to day, exchanging sex for money, there is no other way other than to pick up the ball, literally and metaphorically speaking. The MM gambling arenas are the places to go.

At an MM gambling arena the girls sometimes gamble, but most of the time they shop around, looking for customers. There are several ways for a girl to get a 'date' here. Firstly, she can wear a sexy outfit and put on gorgeous make-up. Then she can browse for potential prey, looking to see if anyone is interested. If, after quite sometime, she still hasn't scored, the girl can spend a while gambling at the MM gambling machines. Some of the girls come both to gamble and to find customers. Others come because they have already been booked. In that case they are usually booked at the karaoke club beforehand, and the guest asks them to go to the gambling area to play before he closes the real deal. Lastly the MM gambling arena acts as a rendezvous point because the client is addicted to gambling.

True, not every girl who comes to the MM gambling arena is looking to 'date' a man. Some call girls come to gamble and try their luck. They sit for hours, sometimes gambling until 4 am. When they realise that there is no luck on the horizon, they take off, not even bothering to wait for some man to ask them for a date.

The MM gambling machines operate twenty-four hours and almost every hour every machine is occupied. Even at 4 am, the atmosphere is far from quiet, with people laughing and chatting. No wonder the MM gambling arenas have become favourite spots for girls to meet up with clients. Even better is the fact that these places are open to the public twenty-four hours and, more importantly, they don't charge an entrance fee.

The Island and MM Girls

Joyce and Wulan are two girls who like to 'operate' around the MM gambling arenas. Wulan is a twenty-four-year-old Indonesian-born Chinese girl. She has fair skin, an oval face, a slender body, a flirtatious voice and always dresses sexily. Sometimes she wears a very low-cut V-neck top or a miniskirt. For her, hanging out at MM gambling arenas is nothing out of the ordinary, especially at CT gambling arena where she is based.

Joyce is twenty-two years old and comes from Palembang. She moved to Jakarta three years ago and is now a regular at gambling arenas. She has a very pretty face, long wavy hair and a sexy body that makes her the centre of attention whenever she walks into a room. It is not uncommon to see Joyce and Wulan team up, walk sexily around the gambling arena, then sit next to each other.

They both work at SA karaoke club as freelance GROs. SA is an internationally acclaimed entertainment hub located near the gambling arena of CT. In fact, CT and SA are located in the same building. For Wulan and Joyce, GRO is only their official title because, as you might know, they offer extra commercial sex services too. The GRO title is used to disguise the fact that they are prostitutes and to make it easier for the club's management. Some use the terminology 'singer' or 'female escort', but their tasks are not that different to those of a GRO. The only difference is that the girls are displayed in the waiting room so that it is easier for the guests to choose which one they want. Some use the term 'dancer', but this type of girl is only delivered to a private room if someone has ordered her directly or through a mammi.

As for a GRO, her daily task is usually to bring as many guests as she can back to the karaoke club where she works. So it is little wonder that so many GROs often end up with clients themselves—they are practically the same as a singer or female escort, namely a prostitute. But unlike a singer or female escort, the action for a GRO takes place after work and outside of the karaoke club. That is why the order for the date usually comes from outside the karaoke club too. So, who would have thought that a GRO was also a prostitute? In terms of working hours, a GRO is more flexible. She even gets the same benefits and monthly pay, based on the number of guests she brings to the club.

Almost every night Wulan goes to MM gambling arenas. If she is not there by herself, she appears on the arm of some man, and usually a different man each time.

'If I get bored at the karaoke club, I go to the MM gambling arena for a change of scenery,' said Wulan when our gambling machines were once accidentally side by side.

'I get bored easily at the karaoke club, especially if there aren't many guests, so I come here,' Joyce also admitted.

The MM gambling arena is Wulan and Joyce's 'playground'. They go there four or five times a week and, of course, their sexy bodies get them noticed. They walk seductively among the crowd of gamblers and, without hesitation, they stop to say hello to familiar faces. Sometimes it is just for a friendly chat, sometimes they subtly ask for money. But the main reason is to get capital for gambling.

But even if they do work as prostitutes, Wulan and Joyce are actually very selective. They only choose people they already know. One time Wulan got so upset because a guest who she barely knew at the karaoke club asked her to sleep with him straightaway.

Unlike the other ladies at nightclubs who usually have certain rates, Wulan and Joyce play in a different league. Their rates are more expensive than average, and almost the same as a high-class call girl who charges Rp2 million (US$240) to Rp3 million (US$360) per date.

It makes sense considering Wulan and Joyce live on the eighteenth floor of quite a luxurious apartment near to where they work. The apartment has full facilities, like a four-star hotel. The rent is Rp2 million (US$240) to Rp5 million (US$600) per month. A lot of girls with the same profession live there too. They often take their clients to their apartment if they have known the clients for quite a while and the clients are their regular customers.

The fact that Wulan and Joyce are Micky Mouse Girls is no secret. There are a lot of other girls who are too. Nowadays, most of the MM gambling arenas are closed, and only a few still open in secret. Many of the MM Girls have gone back to their original haunts: karaoke clubs, discotheques, cafés or clubs. They now work as freelancers at some of the places that offer sex on their menus. Some have moved to massage parlours or beauty salons.

It is interesting to know that MM gambling—which, over the past five years, has played such a huge role in Jakarta's nightlife—is now quite dull. But has it gone for good? No. Some businessmen have tried hard to keep the gambling arenas going by moving to more secluded venues on a small island near Seribu, not far from Jakarta.

And many MM Girls have moved there with them. Like most revivals, gambling arenas have made a comeback and are now even better than before. The girls are prettier, sexier and, of course, more tempting. God only knows how they find them. Every day there are at least five boat trips which bring guests to the island. The atmosphere is different than it was before, quieter and more comforting. And even though it takes longer to get to the gambling place—at least one hour from Sunda Kelapa

Port or Ancol—hundreds of people still go there every day.

The new MM gambling arenas are located among restaurants, cafés, lounges, cottages and an amusement park. And the MM girls are even more willing to 'double up' on their jobs. This remote but well-facilitated place is such a great benefit to the sex industry, giving the industry the opportunity to grow more ... and more ... and more.

The All-In
All-Night Gigolo

Gigolos also spice up Jakarta's nightlife. You can find them at love houses, gyms and beauty salons. Some are involved in high-class practices, while others advertise themselves on the net. The choice of gigolos is endless: from local to those imported from Nigeria, India and even Pakistan.

One morning I read something really interesting in one of Jakarta's daily newspapers. A group of intriguing adverts caught my eye:

'Massage for men and women. A good-looking, athletic male worker. Take-home order. Contact Ami: 0818 1727 ...'

'Massage for women. A professional male worker for hire. Contact Alex: 0816 48503 .../ 08114367 ...'

I also found similar ads, not only in the printed press but also on the net. There are a lot of straightforward gigolo sites. The gigolos on almost every website give their particulars, including details such as their mobile phone numbers. Below are some of the adverts I found on the net:

'Priyo, a twenty-three-year-old, good-looking male. 173/65. Athletic, tanned, ready to serve a lonely girl who lives in Jakarta Pusat. If you are a woman who is willing to spend between Rp500,000 (US$60) and Rp1 million (US$120) (negotiable), please call 08561568 ... between 7.30 pm and 2 am, or email: lekong_xxx@yahoo.com'

'Hansen, a twenty-six-year-old man, 172/75, medium build, fair skin, ready to be a great companion for a lonely woman who lives around Jakarta Pusat. If you are a woman who is willing to spend Rp750,000 (US$90) per night, please contact: 08151863xxx between 7 am and 5 pm. Saturday–Sunday, off. Email: penang_xxx@hotmail.com'

'Andi, a twenty-eight-year-old handsome man, 175/71, athletic, has fair skin, ready to give pleasure to a lonely woman out there who lives around Jakarta Selatan. If you are a woman who is willing to pay Rp500,000 (US$60) to Rp1 million (US$120) per night, please call 081216781 ... between 6 pm and 11 pm or email: lola_xxx@yahoo.com'

The gigolo trend has become more popular due to the fact that more lonely women are needing entertainment. The use of the Internet has made this kind of service even more accessible. But as well as posting on the net pictures of themselves in seductive poses, the gigolos also market themselves via love houses, salons, massage parlours and gyms. Of course the main target is always a lonely woman or a dame with a huge appetite for sexual recreation.

And the trend is now nationwide. For example, The Bali Gigolo Club recently posted on their home page an invitation to whoever might want to join the club:

'This home page is the sequel to the first home page, Gigolo Bali 2000. For those who wish to join Bali Gigolo Club it is very easy. Please register your email address in the space provided. Membership is also open to those who live outside of Bali. Once you have registered as a member you will be informed of the sex-mania activities taking place outside Bali. So for those of you who don't live in Bali, no worry, lah. If you come to Bali, we'll make you happy, lah.'

The gigolo trend is also rising because of an increasing demand from women of every social status: singles, widowers, housewives, working women and playful dames. It seems like gigolos are very aware of the fact that women need to be sexually satisfied. Of course, to fulfil these sexual desires the gigolos must learn several tricks. These tricks come from experience and nonstop learning, which is exactly what gigolos bring to the table: they know how to pleasure a woman. It is a fact of life that a woman finds it harder to have an orgasm during sex than a man. That is what Andy told me too. Andy is one of the gigolos who advertises himself through the net.

On one occasion I called Andy out of curiosity to find out what kind of services he offers, and tips and tricks he uses to satisfy his female clients. The twenty-eight-year-old lad, who had fair skin and was about 175 cm tall, said confidently that he was an expert at handling women who had trouble reaching the big O. That was why, he said, he learnt where the erotic spots were on a woman's body and how to stimulate those spots.

'To really know where the spots were, I spent almost a month learning from my fitness teacher, who is also a massage therapist. He told me there are hundreds of things which a man can do to satisfy a woman,' said Andy. Andy admitted that most of his clients are very satisfied with his services. Some have even confessed that they had never really had the big bang orgasm before meeting Andy.

It was obvious from the way he spoke that Andy was a very confident guy, but at the same time was also sweet. But that was him. He admitted he had been in the profession for almost three years, and that he received at least two to three orders per week through his advert on the Internet. First he and his client agree to meet somewhere, with the new client making the first move. They meet and get to know each other, which is very important for the client who needs to know that Andy is who he says he is in the advert. It is a very crucial meeting.

'The clients need to be sure about who their partner is. If I turn out to be very different from my ad, they will probably say no. And for me it's very easy because I always deliver what I promise,' said Andy.

He charges from Rp500,000 (US$60) to Rp1 million (US$120) per date, but this depends on what is agreed with the client. On average he charges over Rp500,000 (US$60).

'If I don't get Rp1 million (US$120), I will get at least Rp750,000 (US$90). But that's for one night, not for a short time,' he added.

Andy knows that most of his clients are not very good-looking. He says it is unrealistic to hope for a gorgeous, sexy client. Getting a client like that would be like winning the jackpot.

'I try to think practically. If the girl is sexy and gorgeous, why does she need to hire a gigolo? She must have a long queue of men willing to make her happy for free,' he said.

Even so, the gigolos do have some requirements of their own before they accept a booking. For example, if a gigolo offers his services for free he will usually insist that the client is beautiful, sexy, sophisticated, attractive and definitely not a female prostitute. Sometimes a gigolo will also insist that the female client has affairs with other men and, in terms of sexual services, she must agree to have sex in every position, including oral and anal sex.

'But I don't do that,' Andy added. 'If there's no money involved, then I am not a gigolo. It's just a personal affair.'

The All-In Gigolo

There are many different types of gigolos. For example, some choose to be massage boys, call boys or male mistresses. Socially, gigolos are divided into different classes in the same way that female hookers are. Some service the low end of the market, some the middle and others the high end. The classes are categorised according to how much one date costs. For example, a low-class massage boy would have to charge between Rp100,000 (US$12) and Rp200,000 (US$24) per date. A massage parlour near Pasar Rebo charges this amount. Even though it has only been in operation for five years it has been quite successful, despite having only five to ten massage boys.

As for a middle-class massage boy, his rate is between Rp300,000 (US$36) and Rp500,000 (US$60) per date. The massage parlours that set their rate between that range are WN around Menteng and HG salon at Tebet. Both places are like regular beauty salons, but the difference is that the guys who work there offer extra-special treats for the ladies. Yes, sex dates. At both salons there are three rooms that are used as lulur treatment rooms. Lulur is a traditional Javanese skin treatment which consists of massaging, scrubbing and masking the body using herbal oils, a scrub and a masker—but extra treatments are also on the menu.

As for the high-class gigolos, they usually market themselves through networking, a pimp or hiring a special 'events organiser' who often organises parties for jet-setting ladies.

The upper-class gigolos come from many different backgrounds: public figures (actors, models, singers), guys who work at exclusive love houses, and guys who become male-mistresses to very rich women or dames. The transaction is usually very secretive. For example, in the world of celebrity gigolos there is something called a SDC (shopping date, dinner date and check-in date). The system was set up for first-time clients so that subsequent transactions with the client could be easier and less complicated, especially if the client was to become a regular customer. If the client becomes a regular customer, then a long-term affair begins, and the status of the gigolo is upgraded to semi male mistress. However, despite his new status the gigolo will still only charge his clients based on what they order. Rumour has it that an action star—who was famous between 1995 and 1999 and is now a television star—was once a male mistress.

For a gigolo who is involved in a long-term affair, there is one rule he must adhere to: he is not allowed to have a relationship with any other woman, provided that the woman he is involved with takes care of his every need. In most cases these kinds of gigolos are taken care of very well and they live a luxurious life. Another way for a high-class gigolo to get clients is by becoming a male 'trophy' or male stripper for private parties thrown by jet-setting women.

Once, my friend Riany, a twenty-nine-year-old promotions manager for a soft drinks company, asked me to accompany her to a gym in Radio Dalam, Jakarta Selatan. Riany is single and very curious about male gigolos. So, one afternoon I met her at Plaza Senayan and we went to Radio Dalam, about twenty minutes away. The gym was about ten or twenty metres off a main road, located next to a pharmacy. When we got there it looked like a typical gym. Some men and women were exercising, accompanied by their instructors.

Curiosity getting the better of her, Riany confidently approached one of the guys who was wearing a gym T-shirt. He had an athletic body and was one of the staff. I don't know for sure who had told Riany that the gym was the headquarters for gigolos, or indeed that it was where a gigolo and his client met before taking the action elsewhere.

'The rate ranges from between Rp1 million (US$120) and Rp2 million (US$240),' Riany told me. 'Most of the club's members are also the gigolos' clients. A lot of women join the gym just to get access to the gigolos.'

The gigolos stay in a big house near to the gym in Jalan Bangka, Jakarta Selatan. They are mostly from other parts of Jakarta or other areas of Java. The pimp who runs the business there is Prima, a thirty-four-year-old guy who is a little bit girly. He socialises a lot with rich ladies and often attends their events, such as bazaars and arisans, or just goes shopping with them at exclusive branded stores. That is where Prima picks up orders for his boys.

Another gigolo spot in Jakarta is Jalan Jaksa, Jakarta Pusat. The street is crowded on both sides with bars and cafés. It is such a strategic place for gigolos to use to market themselves. Besides Kemang, Jalan Jaksa is also a famous hangout for *bule*s (Caucasians). It has less traffic and the whole street is cordoned off for entertainment.

Jalan Jaksa has now become *the* place to go if you want an imported gigolo, with Nigerians, Indians and Pakistanis being the most popular. The way in which they all try to get customers is very open, with most of them displaying themselves in cafés and bars. They are very proactive indeed. If it is low season and there aren't many clients around, they pose on the big street behind Sarinah Plaza Thamrin, waiting for orders or clients.

If they really have to they will take male clients too. The most important thing for them is that they get money to pay the rent, buy beer, new clothes and mobile phone cards. The rate they usually charge for their services is negotiable: between Rp300,000 (US$36) and Rp500,000 (US$60) for short time, and even lower than that if they are really desperate.

The Sex Market
for Imported Girls

Hundreds of girls are imported directly from abroad. Some come from neighbouring countries like the Philippines and Thailand, while others are from China and India. Some come from much further away, such as Russia, Spain, Uzbekistan and even America. The imported-girls sex market is a vibrant part of Jakarta's nightlife.

The growth of Jakarta's sex industry has been unbelievably fast, and the trends are becoming more outrageous. For example, three years ago everyone was talking about the presence of strippers in almost every exclusive karaoke club in Jakarta. In offices, cafés and malls, guys who were into love sprees would talk about it nonstop.

Nowadays, Jakarta's sex industry has an 'imported-girl fever', and foreign girls are commonly featured on the menus of many triple-X-rated nightclubs. Chinese girls are benefitting the most from this trend. Some clubs have been highlighting them on their menus for some time, but since the fever for imported girls has struck, their popularity has soared.

Of course, the guys who regularly take part in Jakarta's lust trips do not want to be seen as uncool. Just like they don't want to miss out on a fashion trend, they also want to keep up with the latest happenings in the sex industry. Whenever a new trend takes off, everybody starts talking about it. The temptation to have a little taste of it is enormous and the outcome inevitable.

One time, when I was having beers with my four friends in Kemang, Jakarta Selatan, we started talking about the latest sex trend to hit the industry. We all love Jakarta's nightlife and spend most of our time in triple-X-rated clubs.

'Have you tried the Uzbekistani girls?'

'How about the Thais?'

'Or the Chinese girls?'

These questions popped up as we sipped our beers. It had become a typical conversation among night revellers who often gathered to chat about Jakarta's nightlife.

'Not yet. What's so special about them?'

That was the kind of question that would then turn into a long discussion. Then the most experienced guy would, of course, be the one to proudly tell his stories from A to Z. Stories about Uzbekistani girls who have a reputation for having pretty faces and model-like figures. Then there are the Thai girls who are known for their wild, odd sex services. Chinese girls who are famous for their smooth fair skin and slim bodies. And so on and so on.

Sitting in there talking about sexy girls for so long was making us hot so we started to drink more and more. Finally we vowed to have a few night adventures of our own.

Uzbekistani Girls

The fever for Uzbekistani girls first hit Jakarta in early 2003. It all started in club CI, in Kota, Jakarta Barat, which soon became *the* one-stop entertainment hub. At the beginning of 2002 CI—which already had a gambling arena, restaurant, discotheque and karaoke club—underwent a major transformation. It added forty karaoke rooms to the twenty it already had. The rooms were a mixture of penthouses, suites, VIP rooms and standard rooms.

Once the renovation was complete, they hired more LCs. Previously their escorts had been mainly locals, with a few Chinese, Filipino and Thai girls. However, after the renovation the club began to hire a large number of foreign girls: at least twenty Chinese girls, twenty Filipinos and twenty Thais. CI did not stop with the regional LCs, but also imported a lot of Uzbekistani girls to act as its new main attraction. The presence of these Uzbekistani girls started a dramatic change in Jakarta's sex industry. Only a few weeks after they'd first made an appearance, these girls were in high demand—men wanted to taste a little bit of heaven on earth.

The distribution of the Uzbekistani girls was managed by a thirty-six-year-old guy named Alay. He was also Uzbekistani and the one who brought a lot of Uzbekistani girls into Indonesia. His business had also spread to several countries in Asia such as Japan, Thailand, Singapore, Malaysia and the Philippines.

The first time, Alay brought at least fifteen Uzbekistani girls to the CI Club. They were on probation for three months, just like when a company launches a new phone and needs time for brand awareness and customer feedback. That's why, at the beginning, CI's transaction policy was a little bit complicated. The Uzbekistani girls were exclusively available for CI members. The booking process also differed in that clients had to book these girls directly from the mammi or the manager on duty. Strippers and local LCs can be ordered directly from the waiters.

After the initial trial of three months, it then became easier to book the Uzbekistani girls, who were becoming a huge hit in Jakarta's nightclubs. Their popularity was rising, and every night society guys were talking about them.

Out of the first fifteen pioneering Uzbekistani girls in Jakarta, I knew two of them very well. One was called Alena and the other, Victoria. Alena had a slender body and straight brown hair. She was twenty-two years old, 174 cm tall and always looked sexy in her tight outfit. Victoria was a bit plump and about 170 cm tall. She was twenty years old with wavy medium-length hair. She had an oval face and her lips were always seductively wet from her brightly coloured lipstick.

When I met them they had been working for CI Club for almost three months. They were starting to take outside orders from places such as AT Karaoke Club, which is located in an apartment building in Thamrin, Jakarta Pusat. But usually they worked at CI Club every day from 6 pm to 4 am under the supervision of a mammi.

'I prefer to take jobs outside. That way I move from place to place so it's more fun and not so boring,' said Victoria in her broken English and strange accent.

Unlike the local LCs, both Alena and Victoria are still in high demand so they don't really need to sit in the display room for long. They prefer to wait for orders in the restaurant or discotheque, and sometimes they are allowed to sit on the comfortable sofa near to the reception desk.

The Uzbekistani girls never really get a chance to relax since there is always someone wanting to book them. Some of the guests are even on a waiting list. After midnight the supply of Uzbekistani girls is usually very low because some of them are already out on bookings, while others go home out of sheer exhaustion. Victoria and Alena told me that they and the other girls live on the twenty-sixth floor of an apartment in Hayam Wuruk, not far from where they work. In their spare time they love to be alone in their rooms. When duty calls, they can be at work in just ten minutes.

Victoria said that before she was transferred to Jakarta she worked in Japan and Malaysia. So did Alena, who once worked in China and then later spent three months in Singapore.

'Usually we have a three-month contract before we are transferred to another country. It's Alay's job to rotate us,' explained Alena, who spoke much better English than Victoria.

But Alena and Victoria both admitted that they like being transferred to Indonesia better than any other place because the clients are usually very friendly and nice. They said Indonesian men are very polite and never force them to do anything they don't want to do. Alena said that in Japan or China she often gets treated rudely by the guests. When they refuse to do weird sex positions, the clients sometimes become abusive.

'My job is to entertain and give sexual services. I don't do weird stuff,' said Victoria, who had had many unpleasant experiences in Japan.

'Oral sex is normal, but anal sex is way out of line,' Alena added. Victoria nodded in agreement.

That was why they loved it in Jakarta: guests never asked them to do anything weird and were nice to talk to. The girls were able to relax and enjoy their job more.

'I get a lot of tips here too. Huge ones. In Japan or Hong Kong the guests are very stingy, ungenerous,' said Alena looking a bit annoyed.

As well as Jakarta, the Uzbekistani girls are also sent to several of the country's other big cities. Due to such a high demand, Alay had spent the past few months importing at least twenty more girls. As a way to develop his 'business', Alay opened several networks in countries such as Japan, Thailand, the Philippines, Singapore and Hong Kong. In Indonesia itself his 'slimy business' has extended to Surabaya, Bali and Batam. In Surabaya, for example, Uzbekistani girls can be found in MT Club, one of the biggest karaoke clubs in Surabaya.

Besides supplying girls to nightclubs, Alay is also involved in the high-class prostitution business. Through several sub-agents in Jakarta, Surabaya and some of the other big cities in Indonesia, Alay runs an underground prostitution business offering multiple services. He reserves a certain number of Uzbekistani girls to light up private parties in hotels, apartments or clients' private residences.

'Myself and four other girls were once booked for a very huge party which was attended by many high commissioners. The party was at a luxurious mansion and I was paid three times my normal rate,' said Alena. She also told me that during the party she and her friends were assigned as LCs to serve the guests, just like LCs do at karaoke clubs. They had to be very friendly, polite, lighten the atmosphere and, last but not least, give extra services in bed.

Booking an Uzbekistani girl can be quite expensive. Their rate is one of the most expensive sex transactions which take place in nightclubs. In CI Club, for example, a one-time booking which lasts for three hours costs Rp3 million (US$360), excluded tips, rent of the karaoke room for at least three hours and, of course, food and beverages. For three hours the girl will provide a standard service, typical of any LC at a karaoke club: keep the guest company while drinking, chatting and relaxing. And don't expect the girl to be a good singer with a beautiful voice. Some of them have only mastered a few songs: two Indonesian songs, two Mandarin songs and a couple in English.

'Almost all of them can't sing very well. Their voices are so-so, which is putting it politely. But they drink a lot. And when they get drunk they chat more, becoming wilder and more ferocious,' said Wawan, a regular customer at CI Club who runs five stores selling mobile phones and accessories in Roxy, Jakarta Barat.

As for bookings taken from guests outside the club, the rate is double or sometimes even triple. If the booking comes from a regular customer of CI Club or AT Karaoke, the rate is double. But if it is an outside guest who nobody knows, the rate is not only triple but four times more expensive than the normal rate. But it all depends on the deal struck with the mammi in charge.

I also found out that the rate in Jakarta is different to that of Surabaya. At MT Karaoke in Surabaya, the cost of booking an Uzbekistani girl is Rp1 million (US$120) to Rp2 million (US$240) cheaper than in Jakarta. While in Batam the rate is between Rp3 million (US$360) and Rp5 million (US$600) per date. This is much more expensive than booking an LC, which only costs Rp350,000 (US$42) for three hours. The same goes for hiring a stripper for a one-hour show. So if a local LC wants to make big money, she has to go to bed with her client. A sex date ranges between Rp500,000 (US$60) and Rp1 million (US$120). The same rule applies to a stripper.

So it is no wonder the Uzbekistani girls in Jakarta are having a great time. Apart from having friendlier clients, they are also earning more money. I've been told that back in Uzbekistan they are nothing special.

'In Uzbek, for a short date with one of these girls the price is between Rp300,000 (US$36) and Rp500,000 (US$60). Even the best girl wouldn't get more than Rp1 million (US$120),' said Prie, who is thirty-eight years old and works for an oil company. He often takes business trips to Central Asia.

The Rp3 million (US$360) the girls earn in Jakarta doesn't all go to them. Forty per cent goes to the club, sixty per cent to the mammi and her protégés and the tips go straight into the pockets of the Uzbekistani girls.

Chinese Girls

The demand in the sex industry for Chinese girls is also on the rise. Like their Central Asian sisters, Chinese girls are also seen as hip and happening in Jakarta's nightlife. They are still seen as the pioneers when it comes to imported sex girls. Long before the Uzbekistani girls started hitting the headlines, Chinese girls were already there, lighting up Jakarta's clubs and bars.

Chinese girls, who are also popularly known as *cungkok*, are famous for their delicately smooth white skin, slim figures, long straight hair, thin adoring lips and sweet innocent faces. Physically they look quite similar to local girls, but what sets them apart are the services and styles they offer.

China is famous for its traditional herbs and ancient recipes which can give the body great stamina. The Tao mantra is known to make pleasures in bed last longer. It uses breathing techniques, different positions in making love and several tricks to conquer your partner in bed. This is why many men would rather date Chinese girls.

In Jakarta Chinese girls have been on the sex scene for a long time. They were probably second only to local girls. It is well known that almost every nightclub offers Chinese LCs, call girls, singers and dancers. There are two kinds of Chinese girls in Jakarta's bars and clubs. The first are those who have been directly imported from China, and the second are those who were born and bred in Indonesia. Both have been in demand in Jakarta's sex industry at different times.

One girl I met was called Mei Lan. Her beautiful oriental face has made her so famous that in the BE Karaoke and Restaurant in Tomang, Jakarta Barata a long queue of men want to date her. BE Karaoke and Restaurant is famous for offering beautiful oriental LCs.

Mei Lan has a slim figure, is about 170 cm tall and weighs 50 kg. When guests want an LC to sing and accompany them in a karaoke room, she is always their first choice. She has a sexy figure, medium-length straight hair and lovely fair skin. People who see her compare her to the late Anita Mui, a movie star in Hong Kong. Getting a date with the popular Mei Lan can be quite challenging though, especially during the peak hours of between 6 pm and 10 pm.

'Some people book me as early as the morning. I really have to manage my time so that no guests will be disappointed,' said Mei Lan when I met her once in late June 2003. That wasn't the first time I'd visited her. I had been there at least three times before and enjoyed karaoke with her. The room we usually used was standard, with a long sofa, sexy lighting, a coffee table, a TV, an attached bathroom and several other facilities.

When we met Mei Lan had been working at BE Karaoke for almost a year. She'd first set foot in Jakarta just after she'd turned nineteen. She comes from a small remote village in Palembang, so she wasn't directly imported from China. But even though she comes from a small remote village in Indonesia, Mei Lan is easily beautiful enough to become a star in an industry where looks matter.

Her main duty as an LC is not only to keep guests company whilst they are singing, but more importantly to make the karaoke room joyful and lively. But, of course, Mei Lan is not only a great companion in the karaoke room. She is also inundated with offers for sex, both inside and outside the club.

'The terms of the sex date depend on what is agreed with the guest. If they make an offer that is a win-win situation, I'll do it. If I don't like what they offer, I will discreetly say no,' said Mei Lan, who goes by the nickname of Mei.

Anyone who is interested in dating the girls outside the club must first pay a booking fee to the mammi, who can also be the general manager. The payment must be made in full twelve hours before the date. Other than that, the hourly rate is the same as it is in the club. The standard rate for a Chinese LC ranges from Rp100,000 (US$12) to Rp200,000 (US$24). The payment must also be made before the guest and the LC leave on their date.

'But the rate doesn't include the tip if the guest wants extra services, such as a sex date,' said Mammi Min, who has been working there for four years and is in charge of fifteen to twenty Chinese LCs which she rotates every month. According to Mammi Min, customers pay between Rp500,000 (US$60) and Rp1 million (US$120) as a tip for a sex date.

The BE Karaoke room is divided into three different classes: standard, VIP and suite. The standard room is no bigger than twenty metres squared, while the VIP room is about thirty metres squared. The suite is almost forty-two metres squared. The rooms with the most facilities are, of course, the VIP and suite rooms. In the suite there is even an en suite bathroom.

Mei Lan is Chinese but was born in Indonesia, but there are about fifteen other girls who have been directly imported from mainland China. The rate for a Chinese girl born in Indonesia and the rate for one imported directly from China is different.To date a girl from mainland China costs Rp1.5 million (US$180) per date for three hours. For that price guests get a companion in a karaoke room plus a sex date, but the tip is not included. Since it is only possible to have a sex date in the suite room, guests have to book this room, which costs Rp150,000 (US$18) per hour.

Karaoke clubs in every corner of Jakarta offer Chinese girls. For example, there are many similar karaoke clubs in Mangga Besar and Kota. Both these places are full of both Chinese girls born in Indonesia and those imported. Another example is LM Karaoke in Hayam Wuruk, where there are at least fifty Chinese LCs who are young, beautiful and ready to offer the best services inside the VIP rooms. Similar schemes can be found in ST, RJ and SY karaoke clubs, all located around Hayam Wuruk.

It is not just karaoke clubs which offer Chinese girls as their highlight. Some triple-X-rated hotels and massage parlours around Mangga Besar and Kota also have them on the menu. For example, EM Hotel in Kota has a 'plus-plus check-in' package. The plus-plus is, of course, included in the date, and guests can choose between local or imported Chinese girls.

The transaction method is very simple. Guests who are staying in the EM Hotel can go directly to the fourth floor. On the fourth floor there is a café and discotheque, and in one corner there is a huge red curtain. Behind the curtain is a glass wall, and behind the glass wall sit many many girls. It's like a scene from a movie. Guests then pick the girl they desire. If a guest wants a Chinese girl, however, he has to speak directly to the mammi in charge.

'The imported Chinese girls are not in the display room, but we can arrange it if you would like to book one,' said Mammi Feny, who was forty-nine and had worked at the EM Hotel for eight years.

From that point on the guest simply picks the type of room he would like, whether it is a standard, deluxe or suite room. The package for one night with a local girl is Rp500,000 (US$60) in a standard room, Rp650,000 (US$78) in a deluxe room and Rp750,000 (US$90) in a suite room. The price ensures a date of three hours long. As for a Chinese girl directly from mainland China, the price is higher. The average package is above Rp1 million (US$120), including the room rent. As for the tip, Mammi Feny said it depends on the guest.

'It depends on the type of room that the guests picks. The more expensive the room, the more expensive the package,' said Mammi Feny.

In the sex industry in Indonesia Chinese girls outnumber Uzbekistani girls. In almost every corner of Jakarta's nightlife, Chinese girls are available. For example, nightclubs in Pluit and Ancol, Melawai, Jakarta Selatan, Mangga Besar and Kota in Jakarta Barat. The CG Club in Mangga Besar has at least seventy imported Chinese girls who work as massage girls or LCs and, of course, offer sexual services as well. These days CG is the largest club in Jakarta. It is the one-stop entertainment hub with the most facilities and is located in the largest building. But it is not just in nightclubs where Chinese girls can be found. The have also begun to filter into underground, long-term, high-class prostitution rings. Many of them become someone else's mistress for three to six months, or even longer.

Since the network of Chinese girls is so big, there are many agents involved. This is different to the Uzbekistani girls and their agent Alay, who dominates the network for Uzbekistani girls not only in Indonesia but also in other parts of Asia, such as Japan, Malaysia and Singapore.

Local Chinese girls are taken care of by the mammies who are themselves under the control of the club's management. For the girls imported directly from China, there are two main agents who are already famous for monopolising the trade in these girls.

What is even more interesting is the fact that imported Chinese girls are distributed only to high-end nightclubs since they are quite expensive. As far as I know, every year both of these agents import at least two hundred Chinese girls. The two hundred girls are then distributed to exclusive nightclubs across Jakarta, and rotated every three months.

I only know the name of one of these big agents. He is called Bos Lin. I've never met him personally but I have met his men. One of them is called Mister Can. Many of Bos Lin's men, like Mister Can, like to spend their time hanging out in gambling dens such as CI near Kota or MD in Kelapa Gading. It was Mister Can who first told me about the network of imported Chinese girls, a trend which is becoming more and more rampant in Jakarta. Imported Chinese girls have become the main competitors for the Uzbekistani girls, who are also getting more and more popular.

'Two years ago we brought in about a hundred girls a year. But now it is almost two hundred. That means the demand is higher now,' explained Mister Can, who can easily gamble for ten hours straight on Micky Mouse machines or blackjack.

Filipino and Thai Girls

Besides a lot of Uzbekistani and Chinese girls—who are the most popular in many of Jakarta's nightclubs and massage parlours—Filipino and Thai girls are also quite popular. In many elite nightclubs, Filipinos and Thais are the second choice after Uzbekistani and Chinese girls.

Most of the Filipinos and Thais are quite standard to look at, and not that different to the Chinese girls. In many ways Filipinos and even Thais look more unique because they are mixed with a bit of Malay.

In Jakarta's sex industry the number of Filipino and Thai girls is quite small, with some nightclubs only listing a few on their menus. CI Club, for example, is famous for its Uzbekistani girls and has only about ten Filipino and Thai girls. The difference is that the Thai girls are not only working as LCs but also as strippers. And they sure give amazing shows since they are bolder than the local girls. Some even use sharp items as part of their stripping act. I once saw a stripper from Thailand dance while at the same time using a sharp razor to play with her genitals. The show was similar to one I had seen in a nightclub in Pattaya the previous year. That time I had gone there with two friends who worked as travel agents. They acted as my guides for a week, taking me to the red-light districts in Thailand.

But not every elite nightclub in Jakarta stocks Filipino and Thai girls. Of those that do there are at least five to eight places I know of for sure, the most popular being TQ Hotel around Grogol, MS Club in Kelapa Gading and CG Club in Mangga Besar, which has become a goldmine for Chinese girls and a money machine for Filipino and Thai girls.

In TQ Hotel there are at least fifteen Filipino and Thai girls who stand by every day waiting for orders. In this four-star hotel, which is also facilitated with massage and sauna rooms, the girls are the stars. Their main job is to be LCs in karaoke rooms, but most of the time they are willing to perform extra services as long as the price is right. Speaking of price, in TQ Hotel, MS Club and CG Club the rates for Filipinos and Thais are the same as they are for their Chinese rivals. For a date lasting three hours in a karaoke room, where a girl accompanies guests whilst they are singing, the price is Rp1.5 million (US$180). That is for a one-time date without sex services. If a guest wishes to take it to the next stage, he has to pay an extra Rp1 million (US$120). As for the striptease show, the price is Rp1.5 million (US$180) per show. Again, that is just for the show.

Usually the mammi in charge will offer one complete package. For example, for an LC to keep a guest company for three hours, with sex as the finale, the charge is Rp2.5 million (US$300). Some lucky guests are able to negotiate and get a special price.

'But as far as I know, not every girl is open to a sex date. That's why you should really get as much information as you can. The easiest way is to make her drunk, then seduce her, ha ha,' said Sapta, a twenty-nine-year-old lad who works for a multinational company in Gatot Subroto.

So for imported girls in the sex industry in Jakarta that is what it is like. It is an industry which is becoming more and more rampant and dynamic. The addition of imported girls has made the scene in Indonesia more ferocious than ever, with girls looking to grab as much money as they can in this lucrative business.

The Monkey Business of Libido Sprees

If the government were to tax prostitution, how much revenue would they make in one year? The amount would be phenomenal. The 'libido spree' business, which is getting more rampant every day, could potentially make around Rp3 trillion (US$360 million) a year. If you want to know how, read on.

Q : Which is the only industry that hardly ever suffers a recession?
A: The sex industry.

Actually, it's not really appropriate to call it an industry as its activities are completely illegal. And yet it operates like a well-run business. Prostitutes are practically everywhere, from the lowest social classes to high society, in bus terminals, train stations, low-class motels, parlours, saunas, salons, hotels, karaoke bars and clubs. I use the term 'libido spree' to describe the recreational packages which are offered by such places—packages which always result in sex.

The plague of places offering libido sprees has started to spread to other big cities apart from Jakarta, such as Bandung, Semarang, Batam, Medan and other big cities. In Jakarta there is a low-class prostitution zone called Kramat Tunggak. Surabaya is a similar story. In fact, Surabaya is well known for Dolly Alley, the biggest red-light district in Southeast Asia. Yogyakarta is famous for Sarkem, short for Pasar Kembang. In Semarang there is the area called Sunan Kuning. Bandung is famous for Saritem, and Solo is known for its prostitution area in Salir. It is clear that almost every city, large or small, has its own red-light district, also known as a prostitution hub.

The Trillion Spree

Dolly Alley, Kramat Tunggak, Sunan Kuning, Saritem or Sarkem are obviously prostitution areas because the sex transactions are straightforward. Only places used to selling sex can make these kinds of transactions so simply. Plus the location is famous and can easily be found. Anyone wanting to gather data on the sex industry can easily find out how many sex workers are there and how much money they make.

The problem is that in some big cities in Indonesia, businesses offering libido sprees disguise themselves as other businesses. Some pretend to be massage parlours, motels, hotels, sauna, salons, clubs, discotheques and so on. In theory they call themselves entertainment, relaxation and fitness centres, but the truth is that secretly they act as places where sex transactions take place.

While researching libido-spree businesses I discovered some interesting facts. There are a large number of places that are underground, compared to those like Dolly Alley or Kramat Tunggak which are already well known. Take massage parlours, for instance. In Jakarta there are hundreds of them, but only about ten or twenty per cent of them offer massages only, without the sex services. The rest are 'straight to heaven' massage parlours which have sex on their menus. Many massage parlours in Mangga Besar and Kota are like this. Do not expect to find a legitimate massage parlour because, on average, they are places people go for sex.

It is the same story with karaoke bars, clubs, saunas, discotheques, salons, motels and hotels. In Mangga Besar, Kota, Ancol, Pluit and Melawai it is easy to find places with interesting and tempting sex menus.

Recently the libido-spree business has grown dramatically. When well-known venues closed, the trade shifted to karaoke bars, love houses and massage parlours. The growing number of sex transactions taking place in these areas has been enormous. They are fertile places, which is why I think the business should be called the 'wet' business. It is even wetter than the stock market. Even though it is illegal, these places still spring up at an unbelievable rate. Law enforcement officers have tried to shut them down but still they keep on growing. The reason being that this wet business isn't just a huge source of income for the people who trade sex for a living, but the chain is just too long to break. It also provides a lucrative income for certain businessmen and businesswomen, such as pimps and, of course, the business owner. He prefers to remain hidden behind other big players, but gets the biggest cut of them all.

In 1997, when I was working at *Prospek* magazine, I read a book by Terence H. Hull, Endang Sulistyaningsih and Gavin W. Jones called *Prostitution in Indonesia*. In fact, I had written a humble essay on a similar subject, based on my own experiences of collecting the supporting data. *Prostitution in Indonesia* noted how much money was in circulation in the sex business in Indonesia. The amount was an astounding US$3.3 billion, or more than Rp27 trillion. At that time the sex industry contributed 2.4 per cent to the country's gross national product (GNP).

This enormous amount of money was generated by between 140,000 and 230,000 female sex workers—but that was not an accurate figure. According to the book, many girls were sex workers but just not listed as such, and in reality the figure was double. Those girls not listed were the ones working undetected, such as high-class call girls.

That was thirteen years ago, between 1993 and 1994. Since then, with the growth of libido-spree businesses, the industry has exploded. According to data released by the Authority of Social Rehabilitation, in 1997 Indonesia had 72,724 female sex workers who were listed. From that number they estimated that the number of call girls not listed was much much higher.

The number of estimated workers was divided into four classified groups, based on the worker's income and type of work: low class, middle class, high class and upper class. Personally I define the upper class as the 'crème de la crème' class as so few can afford them.

It was estimated that there were approximately 125,000 low-class sex workers. They usually worked around the red-light districts such as Dolly Alley, Sunan Kuning, Saritem, Silir and Keramat Tunggak. At that time facilities in the area were very limited. Most of these low-class girls serviced the needs of their clients for as little as Rp20,000 (US$2.40) to Rp27,000 (US$3.25) per short-time date.

The middle-class sex workers were estimated to total around 123,000 and they charged higher rates. They operated in humble inns, middle-class massage parlours or displayed themselves on main streets in Jakarta, such as in Bulungan, Taman Sari, Grogol, Lapangan Banteng or Monas. They charged around Rp100,000 (US$12) to Rp200,000 (US$24) per date.

The third class was high-class prostitutes, and they were thought to number approximately 42,000. The sex workers of this group could charge from Rp700,000 (US$85) to Rp2 million (US$240) or even Rp3 million (US$360) per transaction, whether it was a short time for three hours or the whole night.

The fourth class was the upper-class sex workers. These were the most difficult to count but they were very well organised and had their own underground network. They made themselves so elusive because their clients were mostly high profile people such as top businessmen and high commissioners. These upper-class girls had different backgrounds: models, actresses, insurance agents, call girls who'd become mistresses, bank staff, secretaries and college students.

For these girls the most common transaction was called SDC (shopping date, dinner date and check-in date). The girls were organised by brokers or pimps who managed their dinners, shopping trips and check-in schedules. The dinner was the initial rendezvous point so that the girl and the client could get to know each other. They would then decide whether the date would have a future. The system was usually applied to first-time customers. The second stage was a shopping trip after dinner. For clients who had booked the call girl before, the transaction was much easier. The SDC system could be applied randomly and not necessarily in order. Usually after dinner and shopping, both parties would check into a private residence, a five-star hotel, an apartment, a bungalow or a cottage.

If a celebrity was involved with booking a sex worker, the date would take place outside of Jakarta, or even abroad. Bali, Hong Kong and Singapore were some of the places which were famous 'love harbours' for wealthy men who liked to book upper-class sex workers for fun or business purposes. The actual rate hasn't been confirmed, but estimates start at Rp10 million (US$1,200)—and the sky's the limit.

It's true that a few years ago it was a little bit complicated to work out exactly how much the sex industry contributed financially to Indonesia, but it is possible to get an idea from rough estimates. If a low-class sex worker has an average of forty customers per month, and she charges Rp20,000 (US$2.40) per person, his or her monthly income would be about Rp800,000 (US$95). Multiply that number by the number of low-class sex workers (125,000) and the result is almost Rp100 billion (US$ 12 million) per month.

The same calculation can be done for middle-class sex workers. Assume that there are 123,000 workers, each servicing an average of forty clients and charging a minimum of Rp50,000 (US$6) per client. The total revenue is approximately Rp270 billion (US$29.5 million) per month.

When it comes to high-class sex workers, the minimum charge is Rp250,000 (US$30) per date. With an average of twenty clients a month, each has an income of Rp5 million (US$600) per month. Multiply Rp5 million (US$600) by the number of sex workers (42,000) and the result is Rp210 billion (US$25.2 million).

If you then add together the revenue for all three classes, the total is Rp580 billion (approx US$67 million). And that's not including the revenue gained from upper-class sex workers.

Let's estimate that there are 10,000 upper-class workers in Indonesia, with an average of ten clients per month, each charging a minumum of Rp5 million (US$600) per date. That means that in one month, one upper-class sex worker makes Rp50 million (US$6,000). Multiply that by 10,000 (the number of workers) and the total revenue is Rp500 billion (US$60 million).

If you then add all the four classes together, the total is a staggering Rp1.15 trillion (US$127 million) in just one month. In a year, the total income from the sex industry could be over Rp13 trillion (US$1.4 billion). I calculated the aforementioned using data from some years ago. If we use the data collected two years ago, the total revenue would be double or triple that, for sure.

(Please keep in mind that the numbers used are based on a *minimum* estimation. For example, the rate for a middle-class sex worker is based on Rp50,000 (US$6), the lowest. In reality the rate ranges from Rp100,000 (US$12) to Rp300,000 (US$36).)

Let's calculate these figures based on the higher rates: Rp25,000 (US$3) for a low-class sex worker, Rp100,000 (US$12) for a middle-class worker, Rp300,000 (US$36) for a high-class worker and Rp5 million (US$600) for an upper-class worker. Therefore the figures would be:

1. If a low-class sex worker makes Rp25,000 (US$3) per client and has an average of forty clients per month, each worker makes Rp1 million (US$120) per month. Multiply that by the number of workers (125,000) and you get a total monthly income of Rp120 billion (US$15 million).

2. If a middle-class sex worker makes Rp100,000 (US$12) per client and has an average of thirty clients per month, she makes Rp3 million (US$360) per month. Multiply that by the number of workers (123,000) and the total monthly income of middle-class sex workers is around Rp365 billion (US$44.28 million).

3. If a high-class sex worker makes Rp300,000 (US$36) per client and she has an average of twenty clients per month, her total monthly income would be Rp6 million (US$720). Multiply that by the number of workers (42,000) and the total is around Rp250 billion (US$30.24 million).

4. If an upper-class sex worker makes Rp5 million (US$600) per client, and has ten clients per month, she makes Rp50 million (US$6,000) a month. Multiply that by the number of workers (10,000) and total is around Rp500 billion (US$60 million).

So in total, the amount generated is approximately Rp1.2 trillion (US$130 million) a month. That means that the potential earnings in this industry could be as high as Rp1.6 trillion (US$180 million)! For me (and I'm sure it's the same for most people), this number is astounding. The sex industry seems to be growing at a phenomenal rate, even triple or double what is used to be. That means it is possible that in a year these figures could be as high as almost Rp3.2 trillion (US$360 million).

Estimating that the industry is double or triple what it used to be is based on the development and growth of the sex industry in Indonesia, especially in big cities like Jakarta, Surabaya, Bandung, Batam and Bali which are continually growing. The number of places which now offer sex packages is getting bigger. As a result, the number of workers involved in the industry is also growing at the same rate.

Legalisation

In a tent café around Semanggi I had a discussion with my friend Ramsy. He is thirty-two years old and works as an accountant for a public company on the BEJ (Jakarta Stock Exchange).

We were pondering the question: if Thailand can make money from prostitution, or so-called 'sex tourism', (and even make it its largest source of income), why can't Indonesia do the same? In fact research shows that the sex industry in Indonesia is as big as the one in Thailand, or even bigger because you can find sex services in almost every city in Indonesia, hidden or not.

Thailand's reputation as a 'country for sex tourism' is not just limited to Southeast Asia, but is worldwide. Just check out travel reviews, such as the one posted by a West German travel agency called Rosie Reisen:

'Muangthai is such a special place and exceeded my expectations, especially when it came to the women of Muangthai. But it is not easy for a foreign tourist in Muangthai to locate the best place where he can taste heavenly pleasures ... Asking in not-so-fluent English where to go for beautiful girls was quite annoying ...'

Another example is sex-tourism advertisements are openly displayed in public. They use seductive phrases such as:

'Slim, beautiful, with glowing tanned skin. These girls love white men in the most erotic and devoted way. They master the art of making love, an unknown art in Europe ...'

Prostitution is legal in Thailand. That is why this wet industry is automatically taxed. According to Thanh-Dam Truong, author of *Sex, Money and Morality: Prostitution and Tourism in Southeast Asia,* in 1986 a total of 2,818,092 people visited Thailand, and the country's income from tourism was 37 million baht (US$1 million). That was in 1986. Imagine what it must be today? Surely it is way higher.

And how about in Indonesia? Taxing the sex industry in Indonesia is still a long way off since giving legal status to sex workers is still out of the question. In reality the sex industry in Indonesia grows like fungus in the rainy season: every time it rains, the industry just keeps on growing.

'So where does all that money go then?' I asked Ramsy.

'To private bank accounts, of course, because it isn't taxed,' said Ramsy.

That was true. I knew from data I'd collected in the field that a sex transaction is not taxed, whether it takes place in a massage parlour, an elite karaoke club or an exclusive nightclub. The only things that are taxed are the room rent and the food and beverages.

Just look at the high-class transactions which take place in 3X Club, AJ Hotel in Hayam Wuruk, Jakarta Barat. The hotel has just launched a new club, which offers extra sex services. The sex workers vary from locals to Chinese born in Indonesia to imported girls. The rate for one transaction is Rp1.5 million (US$180). This transaction is usually called a *transaksi satu setengki*, Indonesian slang for 'half a transaction'. The rate already includes the room rate.

Another example is when I hired strippers in an elite karaoke club in M Hotel around Tomang. The price for watching a sexy dance was Rp450,000 (US$55). The room rent for three hours was Rp700,000 (US$85) and, of course, I had to order food and drinks. When I paid my bill I saw that there was a room-service tax, and a tax on the food and drinks, but the strippers fee was untaxed.

This is true in many places, whether they are massage parlours, saunas or clubs. The same goes for when I paid Rp3 million (US$360) for a sex date with the Uzbekistani and Russian girls, and Rp2.5 million (US$300) for a mount-blow service from a Macau girl.

'If every "purchase" was taxed, the revenue would be enormous. There would be enough money to close the gap between the haves and have-nots, and to build the nation and fight poverty,' said Ramsy with smile.

And it looks like the sex industry will be hip, happening and dynamic for years to come. The problem is that the libido-spree business has never been properly monitored, so the money it generates just goes into the pockets of a few. The question is: is it possible for Indonesia to legalise prostitution? I don't dare to answer that.

'For me, let's just get real,' said Ramsy. 'The fact is the sex industry is here to stay, so why not take advantage of it? But who am I to say such a thing? I am only a stockbroker, ha ha.'

And on that note he said goodbye and headed back to his office where he still had work to do.

The Midnight Lesbian Package

A new marketing technique was introduced to sell a hotel room. Extra sex services after midnight were available to guests. These included sexy massages, shows by cocktail girls and full-service lesbian packages. All of them were discount free.

The hotel also had an interesting tip for those travellers who wished to save a few bucks on their accommodation: check in after 10 pm and ask for the special rate because rumour has it that the hotel staff can give fifty per cent off the official rate. You don't need to be well connected to get this special treatment since it is the hotel's policy and is registered in the computer.

That was also how another hotel gained more customers. A large discount was offered to those who just needed a hotel room to relax in for a little while, or those who needed some place to rest during transit. These were the mobile customers who checked in late at night and checked out early in the morning.

'Nowadays there are a lot of hotels and apartments which apply the official transit rate,' said a friend of mine who often does business with colleagues from out of town. He mentioned RA, HM, WP and MI Hotel in Jakarta Selatan.

In the beginning the transit rate—which used to be known as the *bobo-bobo enam jam,* or 'six hours sleeping rate'—was used in hotels and motels which looked identical to the places offering sexual affairs. Nowadays the question is whether or not the transit rate is going to be used for what it was originally intended.

'Well, it depends on the person,' said my friend. He knows of some hotels which allow the transit rate to be misused right under their noses. In fact, many of them even provide extra sex services.

'There are even midnight packages,' he added. He mentioned RA, HM and MI Hotel as the most popular places among lusty adventurers. RA Hotel, in particular, offers to indulge a man's libido twenty-four hours a day.

Special Packages

RA Hotel isn't part of a reputable luxurious international chain. Located in crowded Jalan PG, Jakarta Selatan, it is a five-storey, three-star hotel that charges between Rp300,000 (US$36) and Rp500,000 (US$60) for a deluxe to suite room. It began operating five years ago and is always clean, unlike an average three-star hotel. The lobby is not very large and the first floor has an information and reception area, a coffee shop, a restaurant, a shop and a beauty salon. The second floor has a fitness centre, a salon and the biggest space is used as a massage parlour. From the third floor up, the rooms have windows which either face the street or overlook the houses nearby. In the basement there is a small discotheque called NA Discotheque, which also shares its space with the car park.

'The massage service is open twenty-four hours,' said Yudha when we arrived at the hotel at around 11.30 pm.

Why don't we get a discount? I wondered. It seems that, in this hotel, the special discount only applies to members. But it is okay because the standard rates are still very reasonable. It is the basic law of supply and demand: whenever the demand is high, the occupancy rate is also high, occasionally over 100 per cent.

'Meaning that at weekends some rooms are used more than once in a single day,' said Yudha.

That was true. We weren't there at the weekend but there was still quite a crowd in the lobby. Most of the people there were young guys, between twenty-five and forty. Some were women in their twenties and thirties. People sat in the lobby, smoking and chatting, while others were in the coffee shop, some near the lift area. The ones who caught the lift down were heading towards the car park, while those who went up were, of course, heading to a room or the fitness and massage centre on the second floor.

The NA Discotheque isn't very big. Its seductive lighting, cigarette-smoke atmosphere and loud beating house music welcome anyone who enters. And just like any other discotheque, it is a place people go to relax and enjoy themselves. When I was there some of the guests were enjoying the music, dancing to the rhythm, elbow to elbow on the dance floor. Others were seated but still moving to the music as they sipped their drinks. In that place it was easy to express your sexuality, and some ladies were using their looks to tease everyone who looked at them.

After a while a middle-aged woman approached us and whispered something in Yudha's ear. According to him, she was one of the mammies and was offering us company.

'Which one do you like? Just tell me,' she said between the ear-splitting music.

Night had fallen but the discotheque remained busy. One or two people left, then one or two came in. Everybody seemed to be enjoying themselves. And another thing that remained the same was that the place was full of the scent of a woman, just like any other nightclub. Some of the women were there not just to have fun but also to make a living selling their bodies and entertaining men in sinful ways.

At around 1 am we went upstairs to a room. From the fifth floor the street below—which was usually heavy with traffic in the mornings and afternoons—was very quite and peaceful. One or two cars passed and Jakarta's city lights glowed, forming a wonderful skyline.

Suddenly someone knocked quietly on our door. A young woman entered, smiling broadly. She was wearing a blue nurses uniform. My guess was that she was around twenty-five years old. She had straight medium-length hair and wasn't beautiful but sure looked attractive. Her body was a bit plump, her skin was fair and she was wearing light make-up. She looked very decent.

'The order is very late. You guys went to the discotheque first, didn't you?' she asked. While approaching the bed she introduced herself as Nina from Bandung.

I then realised that Yudha had ordered a massage girl from the fitness parlour in RA.

'So, do you want a body massage or something else?' she asked matter-of-factly. Anyone not used to this kind of thing would probably find her manner a bit too blunt and shocking. I kept thinking that if the dialogue continues this way it will start to sound like something out of one of those books which are secretly sold in flea markets or hawker centres. But talking this way was what she (the night shift worker) had to do. Even if she didn't always get the response she wanted, it was her job to offer other packages, such as a two-in-one service, a cocktail girl or a lesbian package.

Although these offers sound curiously tempting, I'm sure they are not that different from the standard entertainment men pay for. For example, a cocktail girl's job is to massage the client, but since these girls want to earn extra money, they combine a normal massage with extra, sometimes including oral sex but never intercourse because the rate for that is different. A lesbian package consists of two women acting erotically to turn on a guest, then end with the guest having sex with both the girls. It is also known as the two-in-one service.

There is also an erotic dance show on offer, which is usually available in a karaoke club or bar. A striptease show can easily switch from room to room so that privacy can be maintained and there is the option to pay for extra services.

In RA Hotel these kinds of sexual transactions are added extras. They are separate from the hotel's main fuction, which is to act as a place to stay and rest when away from home. However, although these services are separate, they are surprisingly out in the open.

The Twenty-Four-Hour GM

Management in most of the hotels in Indonesia deny any knowledge that such services exist, of course. Most of the hotel's facilities—such as a bar, restaurant, discotheque, karaoke club and massage parlour—are considered standard in any hotel and are usually run by an outside party. The country's hotel regulations forbid the presence of illegal material, inappropriate and endangering behaviour, and states that guests will be held responsible for all activities that fall outside these regulations.

'So if anything goes wrong, it's not the hotel management that is held responsible,' reasoned a hotel executive. 'We certainly can't check every room without infringing on the privacy of our guests.'

Hotel policy is to stay out of everybody's business, which is good news for those who want to make extra money out of the guests. For example, discotheques and karaoke bars are not just places to chill out in and enjoy the music, but are also places for sexual trading. The massage service in RA Hotel openly operates from 9 am till 3 am and is divided into three shifts. Of course, the late-night service does raise some questions, as does the afternoon service.

According to Yudha there are eight VIP rooms, each costing Rp90,000 (US$10) an hour. A date with a beautiful woman here will definitely end up in sex, especially if it is a late-night massage service where the guest can go from room to room. No wonder sexy services, body massages, cocktail girls and full services are popular.

'What makes it interesting is that here the GM is on standby twenty-four hours,' said Yudha.

GM is the term used for the person who connects the guest with the 'object of affection' by offering different services. Usually the GM is the mammi, who manages the girls in the karaoke clubs, discotheques and bars. It is her responsibility to make the transaction with the guest and avoid rivalry between the sex workers, which can damage the rate system and the system itself. It is difficult to set a rate for a call girl, but they usually go by age and appearance. Older women and average-looking women, for example, can earn between Rp300,000 (US$36) and Rp500,000 (US$60) for one to three hours. The most sought-after women charge between Rp500,000 (US$60) and Rp1 million (US$120).

'That's how they rate the LCs who work in the underground karaoke bars. But those places only stay open till 2 am,' Yudha said.

As well as the official rate, the girls usually ask for tips. Tips depend on both parties. Some women associate tips with certain services and usually charge extra for them. Some of these extra services include 'cat service', 'pussy bath', 'two-in-one', 'lesbian show' and others.

And because there are a lot of girls who try to make extra money this way, rivalry between the girls is inevitable. They secretly get help not only from the GM but also from security staff, bell boys and even team up with the other girls. In order to get as many tips as they can, the security or hotel staff do not hesitate to tell male guests about these extra-special, late-night services.

The result is that the GM is on the go for twenty-four hours nonstop. The massage service officially operates from 9 am till 3 am, so requests received outside of operating hours are not available.

Open Transaction

While some of the hotels complain they don't have enough guests, RA Hotel is always full—and the guests are all there for the same thing. Most of them are men looking for sexy adventures or secret lovers who need somewhere to meet and act out their passionate affairs.

My friend Yudha admitted that he stays at RA Hotel at least once or twice a month. He doesn't exactly 'stay' as a normal hotel guest would, but rather goes there to indulge his lust. He isn't necessarily into sex, but goes there more to find erotic entertainment which is both amazing and mind-boggling.

'These days a lot of strange things are happening,' he said.

Take lesbian packages, for instance. At first it is really hard to believe that an Indonesian girl can do such a thing, and in Indonesia. That's why we said yes to Nina's offer to try it out.

As promised, Nina brought her two other friends, Yeni and Susan. Yeni was twenty-four years old and came from Semarang, while Susan was twenty-five years old and came from Bogor. Their names and origin didn't really matter because the information they gave us was hardly true. It was obvious they weren't new to the business. Susan, for example, had become a call girl in TA nightclub in Tanah Abang. One and a half years later she moved as she couldn't stand being a goldmine for the mammi. As for Yeni, she had also been a call girl in several different places before. Nina had worked as a freelancer in a few motels before working full-time in the massage parlour at RA Hotel. She'd got tired of moving around. In other words, they were all very experienced call girls and there was nothing they hadn't done before. They knew each other well, and often worked together in the same team. So if they did have to be intimate with each other, just like in a blue movie, there would be no hesitation or awkwardness. It wasn't so much that they were used to doing a lesbian act, but more that they were good at acting. Nina, Yeni and Susan were the stars of the lesbian blue movie, but there weren't any cameras rolling. And just like in a blue movie, their job was to turn the audience on and get them ready for the next stage.

'I like this package. It's easy for us since we do it together but the payment is still the same,' said Nina. Yeni and Susan agreed.

But that night none of us wanted to take further action. Nina and Susan protested, but soon expressed their gratitude when they found out that their fee would still be the same. 'Actually there are good and bad sides to it. If the guest has already been satisfied just by watching us, what can we say? Maybe he's just different, you know ...,' she mumbled.

We just smiled. According to Yudha, they hate to let the guests down. If the guests are disappointed they might switch to another girl, which means the girls have lost customers. This kind of rivalry also exists among the girls at the karaoke clubs, who also offer interesting packages at different rates.

'So now you know how unbelievably crazy the nightlife in Jakarta is, right?' said Yudha as we were leaving the hotel. It was 4 am. The lobby was already quiet and there were perhaps only one or two guests still around. But downstairs in the basement the karaoke and discotheque were still open. I saw two women get into a taxi in front of the hotel. I wondered if they were Nina's friends.

Jakarta's nightlife seems to be trapped in this kind of service industry. Money is the only goal, and many hotels have now turned into love houses. According to Yudha, RA Hotel is not the only hotel that allows sex transactions to take place under its roof. It is no secret that some hotels in Jakarta Barat, Jakarta Pusat and some motels elsewhere turn a blind eye to illegal practices. And it has been going on for some time.

The Double-Door Girls Package

There is a three-star hotel where you can book a girls package. It has a huge studio with mirrored walls, and is also popular as a double-door hotel. So what's so special about that?

On Saturday nights I usually prefer to hang out with my friends in the most happening clubs. Some of the places we go to are Embassy and CO2 in Senayan, BC Bar or Hard Rock Café in Thamrin, Mata Bar in Sudirman, Blow Fish in Mega Kuningan or cafés around Kemang, Jakarta Selatan such as Badonci, Jimbani, Shooter and Salsa.

One night three friends from Surabaya were in town. They are called Didi, Momo and Jeremy. So I showed them around. I didn't want to take them to some discotheque or café because it would be too boring for them as they are all used to hanging out in cafés or clubs in Jakarta or Surabaya. So I had to take them somewhere else.

They asked me to take them to a few libido-spree places so I obliged. At first I took them to a love house in Prapanca which had been operating for about six years. It was complete with a collection of beautiful girls costing Rp3 million (US$360) per transaction. Didi was very eager to book one of the girls who was being displayed in the reception area, but Jeremy hesitated since the price was so high, especially as it didn't include room rent or F&B.

'It's too complicated. I like something simpler, one whole package,' said Jeremy, who works for a telecommunications company in Surabaya. He then asked if we could leave. Personally I would have preferred to stay at the love house. Why not? The cosy reception area, which looked like a living room, was furnished with luxurious furniture and beautiful interior design. It was full of beautiful girls and all of them looked sexy and dazzling. They were all as good as top Indonesian models.

But when I thought about it I realised it could turn out to be very expensive. 'Hmm, Rp3 million (US$360). And that's not including the extras. Wow, we could end up spending at least Rp5 million (US$600),' I said. Momo and Jeremy agreed with me, so we left the place and continued 'hunting', going to TV Hotel at Jalan PCR near Pecenongan, Jakarta Barat.

The Rendezvous Restaurant

TV Hotel is very easy to locate because it is on a main road. Along the street there are about four or five three-star hotels side by side. As well as hotels there are a few nightclubs, discotheques, saunas and karaoke clubs.

TV Hotel is next to RO Club and has the best entertainment facilities. There is a hotel, a karaoke bar, a discotheque and a sauna. Compared to other buildings nearby, TV Hotel really stands out and looks far superior. The front yard is quite large and used as a car park.

We arrived at TV Hotel at around 10 pm. There were a lot of cars in the car park at the front of the hotel. Valets were busy trying to manage their flow in and out of the car park. In the hotel lobby I saw some guests sitting comfortably on a beige velvet sofa.

'Where are we going? Why did we come to this hotel?' asked Didi.

'Relax, man. Everything you want is available here,' I said, leading them towards the lifts to the right of the reception desk. Two receptionists, a man and a woman, were busy checking in guests. From the lobby we took the lift to the second floor. The walls of TV Hotel were all painted beige with a blue line down the middle. When the elevator's door opened, the first thing we noticed was a sea of pretty faces and sexy bodies. Some of the girls were leaning against a wall, others were sitting on the floor chatting.

This was how the girls entertained themselves while waiting to be ordered. Not far from where they were there was a Chinese restaurant which glowed under yellow lighting. When we arrived some of the tables had already been taken. I saw some men fooling around, accompanied by sexy and attractive girls. The restaurant had at least ten round tables and four sofas. The tables and chairs were all cream with a flowery pattern in the middle. A male waiter approached us and gave us the menu. Almost all the food available was Chinese.

We sat on the sofa and ordered a white beer, a JD and coke and a plate of French fries. We didn't feel like eating a meal just yet. Then a middle-aged woman wearing a blue blazer came over to us.

'Good evening, gentlemen, would you like company? I have Icha and Laras. They are pretty, aren't they?' she said, pointing to two girls who were sitting in a corner smoking cigarettes.

'Wait a moment,' I said. 'We just want to relax first. If we need company we'll call you, okay?' The lady went away.

We sat there for an hour, looking around. Almost every three minutes girls came in and out of the room via the restaurant door. All of them looked sexy. I tried not to miss a moment. At the table next to us were three guys accompanied by three girls. The girls laughed coquettishly and sat on the guys' laps without hesitation. Sometimes they would kiss, touch and hug their clients shamelessly. At one point one of the guys excused himself and went upstairs with a girl dressed in white. The couple wanted to finish the business in a hotel room. Of course, the rate had been agreed in advance by both parties. It was then that we realised that the three girls were karaoke LCs.

From what I overheard, the group had spent three hours doing karaoke. After that they relaxed and had dinner in the restaurant while, of course, negotiating the price for the next stage: the sex date. From the LCs point of view there isn't any fixed price for a sex date. If an LC is booked in a karaoke club, she charges about Rp45,000 (US$5.50) an hour for a booking of a minum of seven hours. So if you multiply seven by Rp45,000 (US$5.50), you get Rp315,000 (US$38.50) per LC. That doesn't include the cost of renting the karaoke room for three hours and, of course, the tip for the LC.

'Do you want to do karaoke first or do you want to order? I think we'd better order because if we do karaoke first it will take longer. Let's just book the girls here and you guys can check in directly,' I suggested to

Didi and the gang. We'd already drunk at least four huge bottles of beer and a few rounds of JD and coke, Momo's favourite drink.

The woman in the blue blazer came up to us again. This time she offered us karaoke. She said there was a room available and ready, LCs included. The woman was still trying to convince us to choose Icha and Laras as our companions. I shook my head to the offer of karaoke. It was already getting late, being almost midnight. If we decided to do karaoke first, the evening would take longer. That was why I preferred to relax in the restaurant. I figured it was better than going to a karaoke room. The restaurant was brighter and it was easier to pick the girl we desired. The brighter the room, the easier it was to see how sexy a girl really was.

'If the room is too dark, it's just like buying a cat in a sack. We might end up choosing the wrong one,' said Jeremy passionately. I didn't know if it was the lust talking or the beers.

Double Doors

Since it was already getting late we decided to leave the restaurant, even though it was still crowded. At one table some LCs were loyally accompanying their guests and hadn't moved since we'd arrived. Some drunk LCs who'd just entertained clients in a karaoke room were cooling down with a cup of hot tea each.

'Let's go to the display room and have a look.' I led the guys out of the restaurant and turned left. At the end of the corridor there were two halls. The left hall headed to rooms specially set aside for 'massage plus-plus', while along the right hall there was the display room—a room full of glass walls behind which the girls waited. There were a lot of girls in the room and all of them were ready to offer companionship in a hotel room or a room for massage plus-plus. But these girls in the display room were different to the LCs in the restaurant. The main difference was their official rate. The girls in the display room worked on fixed prices, so it was out of the question to negotiate.

There were only about ten girls to choose from instead of the usual thirty. As it was already late most of them had already been booked, or had taken three or four orders and gone home exhausted. The girls work in shifts—the first shift is from 2 pm till 8 pm, and the second shift is between 8 pm to 2 am—so when it is late there are not many girls left. Which was why, by the time we arrived at the display room, there were only ten girls left. Didi and the gang stared at the girls intensely. A guy wearing a neat uniform of a black vest and white shirt greeted us and encouraged us to pick a girl.

'See anything you like, guys?' I asked. 'This is a better deal than you get with an LC. One of these girls only costs Rp170,000 (US$20), including the room. The tip is up to you, as long as it's not below Rp50,000 (US$6).' Jeremy found a girl he liked. She was Number 27. Momo and Didi hadn't decided yet.

'I like that one in the corner. The one with long hair,' Momo said to the guy in uniform. Didi and I still hadn't found one we desired. Fifteen minutes had already passed and Didi was squinting at the girls but still couldn't choose.

'You go ahead,' I said. 'I'll wait in the restaurant. Who knows? Maybe I'll find someone cool there.' I went back to the restaurant. Momo and Jeremy were heading straight to one of the ten special rooms which were located down the left hall. The rooms were next to each other and no different to a standard room in a three-star hotel. Each was fifteen metres squared with a bed and a shower. There was a mirror on the wall and two bottles of mineral water on a small table.

When I got back to the restaurant it was quieter. Only one table was occupied by two men and six girls. One of the guys was wearing glasses, a polo shirt and a pair of trousers, while the other one was wearing jeans and a stripy shirt. They seemed to be enjoying themselves, laughing and joking. Didi and I sat near to their table.

Oh my god! Suddenly I realised I knew one of the girls who was sitting with the two guys. She's called Leni, and as soon as she saw me she came over to our table. She's twenty-two and comes from Cirebon. I often meet her in cafés such as BC Bar in Thamrin, Jakarta Pusat or in Untitled at the JW Marriot Hotel in Mega Kuningan.

It's no secret that lately, most of the 'date girls'—either those who work as LCs, massage girls, call girls or are residents in love houses—have started to expand their territory by visiting happening cafés and discotheques. Just by looking at them it is hard to tell if they are working girls or clubbing girls as both dress very similarly. For example, I've known Leni for six months and every time I meet her at a club she always looks so trendy. Sometimes she's wearing tight trousers with a short tank top which exposes her belly. She has a little ring through her belly button which makes her look even more stylish. That night she was wearing a purple dress, a pair of high heels and her hair was tied up into a bun. She had light make-up on and the maroon lipstick made her look older. I guessed she was working, accompanying clients.

'Hi, what are you doing here? Oh, you're looking for a girl, aren't you?' she teased as soon as she sat down. Before that she'd greeted me with a kiss on the cheek. I could smell that she was wearing the perfume Premier Jour Summer by Nina Ricci.

'No,' I replied. 'I'm just showing round my friends from Surabaya.'

'No kidding? It's okay, you can be honest with me. Don't be shy,' she teased again.

'Leni, this is Didi.'

'Hi. I'm Leni. Nice to meet you. Have you found a date yet?' Leni shook Didi's hand and smiled.

'Not yet. Haven't found anyone I like. Can I date you?' Now it was Didi's turn to tease Leni.

'No problem. It's not a big deal,' Leni boldly replied, challenging Didi. Then she told us what she got up to at TV Hotel. In a typical week this girl with dimpled cheeks works for five days. Just like the LCs in other nightclubs she is controlled by a mammi. The fact that she is an LC makes it easier for her to network with guys she's already dated, including those she's had sex dates with. As she talked I could smell alcohol on her breath and assumed she was a bit tipsy. No wonder she was talking so boldly. She was also smoking a Capri cigarette nonstop, blowing the smoke out as she talked.

She said she had just accompanied some guests in a karaoke room and, as usual, she had spent the last three hours not just as a singing buddy but also as a drinking buddy. And Leni wasn't alone. She had two other girls with her since there were two male guests. She said that she wasn't feeling a connection with the guests which is why, after the three hours of karaoke was over, she'd ended the date.

'I'm sorry but I'm a bit tipsy,' she said.

Didi smiled at me and signalled that he had a crush on her. I smiled back at him to let him know that I didn't mind.

'Leni, would you like to accompany my friend to a room? Poor boy, he sleeps alone,' I said.

'Really? But I must let you know that the minimum fee is Rp1 million (US$120). It's already dawn too.' She tried to negotiate and Didi didn't care. The rate for a sex date with a standard-class LC ranges from Rp500,000 (US$60) to Rp1 million (US$120). Those LCs who are most in demand charge more than Rp1 million (US$120) per short-time date.

'Okay. You go upstairs and check in. You can check out tomorrow afternoon. I'll wait for Momo and Jeremy.'

Didi finally disappeared with Leni through the restaurant door. This smiley girl looked happier than before. It was already 1.10 am and Momo and Jeremy showed up twenty minutes after Didi and Leni had taken off to their love bed.

The term 'Double Doors' is actually the nickname for TV Hotel and its libido lovers. The first door is for genuine guests who want to check in and have a place to sleep. The second door is for call girls who are on standby for twenty-four hours and can enter those rooms allocated to them in the hotel.

'Oh, that is why it's called Double Doors!' said Momo, who was glowing after his session with his girl.

The Cat Bath
Super Massage

Relaxation. Everybody needs that. One type of relaxation place which has plagued Jakarta is the massage parlour. You can find massage parlours in every corner of the city. There are more and more every day. It seems like, in Jakarta, the need to relax has become so urgent and such a top priority for many people.

These days office workers work so hard from morning till late afternoon that they start to search for any form of relaxation which not only refreshes their minds, but also strengthens their physical fitness. Massage parlours give them just that, which is why they are now *the* places to go to relax.

However, not every massage parlour in Jakarta is practicing what it should. What they are supposed to do is offer standard massage services, such as traditional massage, shiatsu massage, Thai-style massage and many more. But in reality some massage parlours just call themselves this to disguise their seedy business. They put up signs claiming to be massages parlours, but in fact what they are really selling is sex. Sad but true—these kinds of massage parlours offer a whole lot more than traditional establishments.

I did a rough count of how many non-legitimate massage parlours there are in Jakarta and I came up with at least two hundred, spanning every corner of the city: Jakarta Barat, Timur, Pusat, Selatan and Jakarta Utara.

Money As a Guarantee

Rivalry amongst non-legitimate massage parlours is so fierce that each of them try to offer something 'distinguishing' to set them apart from their competitors. One of the most popular things on the menu is the cat bath service. Just reading that made our imaginations run wild as we fantasised about taking showers with massage girls. But that wasn't it. It was just another name, a term, nothing more than the usual foreplay given by massage girls everywhere.

There are two massage parlours, MD and HP in Grogol Jakarta Barat, which are famous for giving a cat bath service. They are located not far from a shopping mall where you can always find men craving fast love.

At around 10.25 pm one night I was with my friend Eko. He's twenty-eight years old and works for a mobile-phone company. We were driving towards Slipi. After about fifteen minutes we reached a big mall and turned left. After parking the car we walked for about twenty-five metres and found a side street off the main road. That is where MD and HP are located.

Both buildings are opposite each other. They have operated for years and never run out of guests. From 8 pm that night the car park in front of the massage parlour was already full. A few discotheques were scattered nearby, making the area a lot more lively.

'Are we going to the discotheque first or are we going straight upstairs?' I asked Eko.

'I think it's best if we have a drink in the discotheque first while we pick our dates,' Eko answered with a grin.

Besides having being a massage parlour, MD and HP also have bars and discotheques on their ground floors. That is where the guests usually hang out first, listening to up-beat music and drinking cold beer. These areas are also display rooms for the massage girls who offer that little bit more. For example, if a guy wants a date, all he has to do is take his pick from the vast number of girls in the room who are also searching for a one-nite stand. As the girls wait for orders they go to the discotheque, looking for prey. The modus operandi is so easy that if a guy finds his mate he can just take her up to the massage parlour on the first or second floor—a massage parlour which also acts as a place for short-time sex.

It seems like in both places the discotheque and massage parlour act as one, each side complimenting the other. For first-time guests who are not yet members, the discotheque acts as the place where they can shop around and choose a massage girl to date. As they listen to the music they are able to chat and drink a bit before the sex transaction takes place. It is the perfect display area. Any guy who wants a sex date doesn't need to waste time figuring out which girl to hit on. All girls who dance, talk and enjoy themselves there are massage girls who offer more. You can forget about finding genuine female guests there, all the guests are men.

Two girls sitting at the front of the disco approached us. The music kept playing and some of the guests were dancing on the dance floor.

'Do you want some company?' one of the girls, who was wearing a black T-shirt and a miniskirt, greeted us.

'Of course, it's our pleasure,' said Eko, and he invited the girls to take a seat. It is easy for guests to blend with the massage girls, who are all waiting to be booked. They drink, dance and, when a booking finally comes in, they land on some bed on the first floor.

Inside the discotheque there are two electronic boards which constantly display numbers in red. The first board hangs near the entrance, and the second board is near the bar. The numbers displayed change every minute and correspond to a girl. When her number comes up she has a booking. The girls wait in the discotheque, dancing with guests until their number flashes. Then the girl will go to the first floor to fulfil her assignment.

But don't expect to find a comfortable room, like in a hotel. In both of these massage parlours the rooms available have air-con but are still not as good as those in a hotel. A standard room is like a doctor's surgery separated by curtains. The VIP rooms are much more comfortable as at least they have their own doors.

Most of the massage girls are local and from outside Jakarta, mainly East Java, West Java or Central Java. And don't expect to find a legitimate massage parlour offering traditional massage, shiatsu massage, lulur massage or even Thai massage. If that is the kind of massage you are looking for, then MD and HP are definitely not for you. All they offer are sex services, nothing more.

The guys who regularly go to MD or HP don't usually need to go to the discotheque first. In the reception areas on the first and second floors—where the sex massage parlours are—there are pictures of girls with numbers underneath. The numbers identify the girls and are their booking codes. If a girl accepts an order, her number is turned face down. When she is available, her number faces up.

Both MD and HP are not regulated by the authorities. They operate from 3 pm till 2 am, but the night shifts are always the busiest. Their reputations as massage parlours which offer sex are not a secret. That's why a lot of men go there at night looking for a human blanket to keep them warm.

In the MD massage parlour there are at least a hundred and fifty girls who work every day, while in HP there are around a hundred massage girls. The rate they charge is pretty cheap for a guy who earns an average wage of Rp1 million (US$120) per month. For example, a standard room costs only Rp50,000 (US$6), and is only Rp40,000 (US$3.80) at HP. The VIP room at MD is Rp50,000 (US$6) per short time. As for a massage girl, the rate is Rp125,000 (US$15) for a short-time sex transaction. The tip is up to the guest.

Imagine, with between Rp200,000 (US$24) and Rp300,000 (US$36) a guy can get himself a date for the night. No wonder both these places are always full of men craving fast love. They are the perfect places for a guy who wants something flexible, simple, affordable and who doesn't want to go through a pimp or check into a hotel. Just make a trip to the extra-service massage parlour and you can have short-time sex and leave in a couple of hours.

Even though a client pays Rp175,000 (US$21) for this kind of service, not all the money goes straight to the massage girl. It it split between four parties: the first share of Rp75,000 (US$90) goes to management; the second share of Rp25,000 (US$30) goes to the pimp or mammi; the third share is security money of Rp5,000 (US$0.50); and the remaining Rp70,000 (US$8) goes to the massage girl. However the massage girl doesn't receive her share on the same day as she earns it. For example, if Rini serves four guests in one day she will earn four times Rp70,000 (US$8) which equals Rp280,000 (US$32). But this isn't the amount that she sees. Instead, every day she gets Rp12,500 (US$1.50) in cash for every transaction she makes. The pimp or the mammi looks after the rest as a guarantee the girl will stay. She is only allowed to use this money if she really needs it.

'The money is saved by Mammi so that we don't spend it on something we don't really need,' explained Rini, who has worked at MD for almost a year. 'We can get our money after two or three months, but only if we need something.'

According to Rini the money is kept by the mammi as a guarantee, preventing the girls from running away to another place. She said that sometimes massage girls would take off from the massage parlour because they just can't stand it any longer. Sometimes they take off with some guy and then become his mistress.

'The most popular girls in here don't usually stay long—three or six months maximum. There's always some guy who'll take care of them instead. Unfortunately I'm not one of those girls so I just take whatever I can get,' said Rini honestly.

The Cat Bath

MD and HP are not the only massage parlours that offer conventional sex packages—meaning they only give regular sex services without any new or tempting services. By contrast other massage parlours, such as BM in Hayam Wuruk, offer a sex menu that is very seductive, especially for guys who love to take lust trips in the city. At BM and RS massage parlours, which are situated close to a big junction near Mangga Besar, the cat bath service is their speciality. This special sex massage has been their secret weapon for years. Both massage parlours are near to each other, and morning, noon and night they are never quiet.

We arrived at 7 pm and could hardly find a parking space because it was already so crowded. Luckily for us someone left and we took their space.

'It's hard to find a parking spot here,' said my friend Eko while closing his car door. 'The street is not big enough for all the guests who bring their cars.'

In BM and RS there are bars which act as rendezvous points for guests who wish to chill out and relax. When we arrived there were a lot of massage girls dressed in green blazers sitting comfortably on long sofas. Some of the mammies or pimps who were coordinating them were busy greeting the guests and showing off their protégés. The bar areas had quite dim lighting in contrast to the room where the massage girls were hanging out. That room was quite bright so the guests could easily see the girls before choosing which ones they wanted to date. Some of the guests who'd already got their dates were going upstairs to the first and second floors. On those floors there are a lot of standard rooms, all side by side along one long corridor. Inside each room there is a bed and a bathroom with a shower. The bedsheets are covered with white linen.

'Cat bath, hmm, I wonder what that is?' I said, trying to imagine what it involved.

'Yeah, right,' Eko replied. 'Like you've never tried it before. It's like a cat licking its food, the only difference being that the cat is a beautiful girl. Go on, imagine how it's done.'

Cat bath is the term used to describe a sex service where a girl licks something, just like a cat, making sure no spot is missed. Actually the service is more like foreplay, ending up more like a short-time sex date. Not every massage parlour has the cat bath service on its menu, and those that do have a competitive edge.

This kind of service is not expensive either. To get the cat bath package the guest has to pay around Rp250,000 (US$30) to Rp300,000 (US$36). The price includes the room rent and the massage girl, so it is no wonder that BM and RS massage parlours are never short of customers.

'C'mon man, let's go home. The water is not working, so the cat bath has been cancelled,' I joked when I saw Eko starting to get intimate with his date.

The 36B Super Breast Massage

There is a new treatment aimed at indulging men by giving them a body massage on a waterproof bed full of bubbles.

At the junction which connects Kota to Mangga Besar, I made a U-turn. It was around 7 pm and there were traffic jams everywhere. I steered my Wrangler Jeep to the left side of the road and down a dark alley. A valet in plain clothes guided me to a car-park space right in front of a shop which sold all kinds of different snacks. Other cars had parked along the same row, and in the corner I could see hawkers selling food and drinks. The alley itself was a dead end surrounded by shophouses. Crowds of people hung out on both sides of the alley, and it seemed like an entertainment hub. I noticed there were about ten to twelve massage parlours there. Blaring out was Dangdut music, an Indonesian folk music rooted in Malay.

I walked slowly, trying to find the massage parlour I wanted. Above the shophouses I read the names BRL, BCL, TNT, MXC and others. I stopped outside the house with the name RS. A middle-aged man wearing a hat and a T-shirt approached me.

'Do you want a massage, boss?' he asked me directly. 'Go ahead. If you want some ABGs, there are some inside.' ABG is the informal term for teenager.

'No, actually I am looking for KT. Do you know where it is?'

'You are in the wrong alley, boss. You should go to the next one.' He pointed to the next alley.

So I walked to the alley he'd pointed to and saw similar scenes. The whole place was full of massage parlours, only there were fewer here than in the first alley. Outside some of the shops, women were standing offering their services to men who passed by.

'Please, sir, please take a look. We guarantee you'll have a good time,' offered a middle-aged woman who was standing in front of one of the shophouses. She was wearing a black suit. 'Please come here, we have a lot of new stock.' As I carried on walking I heard the same invitation from the other women along the street. It was their duty to invite as many guests inside as possible. Their job was the same as the GROs who work in nightclubs, cafés, discotheques, lounges and restaurants.

After searching the area for a couple of minutes I finally stopped in front of the building at the end of the alley. It was the massage parlour KT. A woman welcomed me. Aha, I thought, this is the place I am looking for. Lately KT is the night spot everyone is talking about. It has been operating for years and is famous for its special sex massage service. People call it the super breast massage. It is like a body massage, meaning that the masseuse doesn't use her hands but her body to do the massaging.

36B Super Breast

When I entered KT it was already 8.14 pm. The place was rather illicit. The first thing that caught my eye was the bar. I sat on one of its high chairs and ordered a white beer. On the left side of the bar there was a long sofa and with bright lights. This was the display area. A lot of girls were casually sitting on the sofa, scanning the bar area. It would be easy for a guest who walked into the bar to see the girls here, and he could easily choose his date.

On the right side of the bar there was a waiting room with seductive lighting that looked like a mini restaurant. Some guests were hanging out there accompanied by a few girls. Music was still playing loudly. It wasn't the usual RnB, garage or acid jazz, but instead Dangdut. Sometimes a few disco tunes would come through, but mainly it was Ronggeng Disco. Ronggeng Disco is a type of disco music that is no longer considered fashionable as it is so old and out-of-date.

For a moment or two I just sat there, quietly looking around the place until a mammi approached me. As usual, the mammi got straight to the point, offering me her protégés.

'Which one do you like, boss? Would you like me to pick one for you?' she offered. In the blink of an eye, she came back with a girl who had an oval face, medium-length hair and quite dark skin.

'Please, have a little chat. Get to know each other first. If you don't like this one, you can always switch. This is Nina. She is twenty-three years old,' explained Mammi.

The introduction process began. Nina served me at the bar like a waitress. She poured my beer, made conversation and so on. But I still couldn't help looking around. I couldn't stop thinking about the super-breast girls, the girls famous for their large breasts. Nina, who came from Indramayu, said there were only a few girls in KT who had a bra size of 36B.

'What matters the most isn't the size, right? It's the service,' said Susan, another girl who was sitting at the bar. She was sipping an isotonic drink and told me the drink keeps her active. She'd been sitting at the bar since 5 pm that afternoon and said it was easy to get tired.

'Have you been here before?' asked Nina.

'No, this is my first time. The super breast massage, what is it like?'

'Ah, how come you don't know about that? It's massaging the body using body and ... breast, of course. You'll find out later. Or would you like to try it now?' she asked very directly.

'Let's just wait a moment. Let's have a drink first.'

We chatted for another fifteen minutes, during which time I found out more about Nina and KT. Nina had only worked at KT for a year and, at first, was only freelancing at some nightclubs providing sex services. A mammi coordinated the circulation of the girls. Nina had become a call girl in TC Club in Mangga Besar. Her working hours were flexible and she didn't need to work every day.

'I worked for maybe two or three hours, had one or two guests and then I went home. The mammi got twenty-five per cent as commission from every guest. That's all,' said Nina.

Then Nina decided to settle down at KT because the place was crowded every day. The rate was around Rp250,000 (US$30) per short-time date (not including the tips from the guests). In one day she could service at least two or three guests. For Nina, that was enough to cover all her daily expenses. She could earn between Rp3 million (US$360) and Rp5 million (US$600) per month.

'If I am lucky, I can get five to six guests a day,' said Nina.

She admitted that the guys coming to KT are usually after the super breast massage. Almost every girl who works at this massage parlour gets proper training so she can perform this special unique service well, unlike other massage parlours near KT which don't always provide the service. So even though there are other massage parlours which also offer sex services, KT is still the most popular place.

'Let's go upstairs. It's already 9 o'clock. Don't you want to be more relaxed?' asked Nina. We'd already chatted for more than half an hour and I'd already drunk at least four pints of beer. Some of the guests who'd arrived at the same time as me had already finished the transactions with their dates.

Nina took me to the first floor. KT is not a glamorous place, unlike those nightclubs or massage parlours in some four-star hotels. The exterior of the building is far from luxurious, and there is certainly no interior design. The first floor looks narrow because there are ten rooms located side by side. Nina told me there are also ten rooms on the second floor. On every floor there is a cleaning service which also provides condoms for the guests. A typical room at KT is very basic, a bit like a room in a doctor's clinic or a student's rented room. Inside each room there is a shower separated by curtains and a bed without sheets—and it's the bed that makes it interesting. It looks like it has a leather covering and is waterproof. For guests who don't want a 'body massage', the cleaning staff will provide white linen sheets.

Even though the room Nina and I had wasn't luxurious at all, it did have air-con and the lighting was a bit seductive. The first thing Nina did was take a shower and rub soap all over her body.

'Are you ready?' she asked me when she came out of the shower naked. She covered the bed with bubbles and the super breast massage began. It seemed like Nina was doing erotic and sensual moves, our naked bodies meeting in the bubbles. I felt like a king being served by his sexy concubine.

As it is a sex massage, don't expect to come out from the parlour feeling healthy. The massage given in KT is not about your fitness, but rather a super breast massage that ends up with intercourse.

The truth is that the super breast massage is only foreplay before reaching the real deal. It is interesting to note that the super breast massage service given by KTs girls is a complete package. The charge of Rp250,000 (US$30) includes a super breast sex massage, room rent for one hour plus soft drinks. The tip is a separate issue between the guest and the girl. As for condoms, the guests have to buy them themselves as they are not complimentary. Of course, the price charged by hotel staff is much higher than the average retail price.

'So, what do you think? Any comments on the super breast massage?' asked Nina when we were seated back at the bar. I smiled at her. It was already after 10 pm and KT was about to close.

'We are closing,' Nina explained. 'The last order is at 9 pm. After 9 pm we don't take any more orders.' The bar was now quieter than before. Only a few couples were still hanging out intimately, and some massage girls were ready to go home. I was the last guest to leave. At 10.25 pm I was already back in my car, driving along Hayam Wuruk.

The Taste
Of Massage Boys

It is common to have services which indulge men, but women can also enjoy such pleasures. Massage boys are available on the spot or can be ordered by phone.

' *I have worked for two years as a massage boy. This isn't my only job. I work at the parlour so that I have a place to hang out every day. I also work part-time and take outside orders by phone. Sometimes I get jobs through my pimp. Even though I only get a few orders from outside the parlour, I can charge more. Mostly the guests who order me are women. The guys prefer to come to the parlour directly. I have at least one or two male guests. I get between three and six orders from women every week ...*'

That is Frans' confession. He is twenty-six years old, has an athletic body and works daily in DR massage parlour in Cikini, Jakarta Pusat. The parlour is located near a school famous for art and literature, down an alley on the RS road. The not-so-long alley, which connects Salemba Raya, has at least three massage parlours. Calling themselves massage parlours is, however, a lie as they are all running prostitution businesses. They are all located in the same four-storey shophouse so they are close to each other. As for the DR Massage Parlour, it is in the basement of a three-star hotel. It isn't very hard to find.

The night I met Frans I went by myself. He'd invited me to take a look at where he worked. I have known him for quite a while and never once thought he was a massage boy.

I first met Frans six months before in Menteng, at a hangout along HOS Cokroaminoto Road. There are a lot of hawker stalls there and they are open twenty-four hours. It is the place where clubbers go to relax, rest, sober up or grab some supper from the many delicacies sold there. I met Frans for the first time one Sunday night at around 3 am.

That morning he had been in the Moonlight Discotheque in Kota. The Moonlight Discotheque, which is also known as ML, is a famous rendezvous point for the gay community. Frans told me he goes there regularly at weekends.

'It's refreshing after I've busted my arse off,' he said that Sunday morning while eating a plate of fried tofu dipped in peanut sauce. Frans is the kind of guy who can mingle easily with anyone he's just met, and he always talks very directly. So when he lightly asked me to find him a boyfriend, I said yes but didn't promise anything. Jokingly he then invited me to see where he worked.

Massage Girls and Boys

When I took Frans up on his invitation he was a bit shocked. I met him at around 9 pm. He told me the parlour is open twenty-four hours but there are only a few massage boys and girls who work after 10 pm.

When I arrived, a receptionist greeted me. Then she handed me two albums. The first album contained pictures and details of all the massage boys, and the second album, of the girls. I just kept turning the pages over and over again. There were twelve massage boys and fifteen massage girls. Some of the pictures showed the full body while others only showed half. I found Frans' picture on the second page.

'Could you get Frans for me, please?' I asked the receptionist. Frans appeared five minutes later and looked a bit surprised. He hadn't expected me to really visit him, but before arriving I'd already called him to make sure he would be there.

'Oh my god! I thought you were only kidding,' he said when he saw me. I laughed. We chatted in the reception area.

'But I didn't bring your order. I've been trying to find you a boyfriend, but haven't found anyone quite good enough,' I joked.

'It's ok. I'm just surprise you showed up,' he said.

I wasn't the only one who'd come that night. In the reception area sat two or three other guests, all men. The first guest had already taken the action further and gone inside a room with his date. The second guest, said Frans, was a regular customer who came at least once a week. At first glance I would never have guessed that such a sturdy and macho-looking guy would have booked a massage boy.

'We have a lot of regular customers. I have two myself,' said Frans.

Frans took me to the hotel's lobby on the first floor. At the coffee shop I sat in one corner. It wasn't too crowded there, only five tables were occupied. Some were couples while others sat in small groups. The DR Hotel is a transit hotel which is usually used as a meeting point for those couples who want to have a one-night stand. The hotel is strategically located, being a little bit hidden. Plus the room rate of Rp200,000 (US$24) to Rp300,000 (US$36) isn't expensive so the hotel is always full of guests. It also has a discotheque and a karaoke room.

Frans ordered a cup of hot tea and I ordered my regular drink: white beer. We talked for a while, mainly about the friends we hang out with who often show up in Menteng. We also exchanged the latest news from the nightclubs before moving onto the subject of the DR. By then it was almost 10 pm.

The first thing I asked Frans was how much it costs for a massage boy or girl. He told me that, in the beginning, DR Parlour only provided massage girls for male clients and was open twenty-four hours. Massage boys were brought in one and a half years ago. On the surface, DR says it offers massage services but in reality it does sex transactions.

So not long ago DR began taking women as clients and the massage boys could be hired by female guests. But Frans told me that female guests hardly ever want the transaction at the parlour. They prefer to book a massage boy in a more private place, like their home, an apartment or a hotel.

Frans, who has already been in the 'plus' massage industry for two years, has a lot of interesting stories to tell. The reason why he dipped into this industry is simple.

'I like to massage a guy's body, so I'd rather make money out of my hobby. And it turns out the money is good too, ha ha,' he confessed, laughing. Frans said that obviously money was also one of the reasons why he continued to stay in this line of work.

'I'm not a hypocrite, you know. Of course *duta* (money) is the main reason. Who says you can live without food and nice clothes?' he said lightly. *Duta* is a word that was first used by the gay and transvestite community, but now it is a hip and cool word used by youngsters.

Actually, I told Frans that if money was the only factor, he could find himself a very rich boyfriend. But Frans was left traumatised by his last relastionship. His rich jealous boyfriend made him a virtual prisoner and he lost his freedom. Besides, he told me he gets bored when he only has one partner, that's why he keeps working as a massage boy.

The AC–DC Job

It all began when he met some gays who were hanging out in Moonlight. Through them, Frans gained access to the gym in Radio Dalam. It is not only a health and fitness centre but also a place for relaxation. Inside the gym there are rooms comfortable enough to use for dates. The guests are not only men but also women. Most of the massage boys in the GP Gym are bisexual, meaning they are open to both men and women. Frans himself only takes orders from male clients.

Frans comes from Jakarta and is the youngest of three children. His father comes from Malang and his mother from Purwakarta. He first realised he was gay when he was still in junior high school. Even though he didn't dare express his sexual preference, he could sense that his urges were increasing. When he was in high school, Frans started to express his gayness by attending some love-spree places which offered male sex workers.

'I can clearly remember that my first time with a man was in a massage parlour in Pasar Rebo. I paid him Rp100,000 (US$12),' Frans confessed.

From then on Frans started to meet guys like this. He started to go clubbing in places where he knew gay people would be: discotheques, cafés, lounges and bars. After he graduated from high school, he took several part-time jobs. He worked as a waiter in a restaurant, then he worked in a supermarket, then in a salon. He was trained to give lulur and cream-bath massages when he was working at the salon. But he got bored with the company's strict policy and finally decided to open his own business. As he didn't have enough money, Frans took a short cut and became a call boy. At first it was only for fun but then he got used to it.

'It is so practical. You not only get a date but also money,' he reasoned.

As well as being a call boy, Frans also freelances for a pimp. He works per transaction, and is allowed to take orders from other pimps or work by himself. Some of his friends act as the go-betweens.

'I have friends who are also the go-betweens for every transaction,' he said while smoking his favourite cigarette. Even though nowadays Frans works regularly at the parlour, he can still take outside orders on his days off or after working hours.

Since the beginning Frans has strictly maintained that he doesn't take orders from female customers. He says that is something he really can't deal with. Three or four of his colleagues at GP Gym are bisexual, or AC–DC. (AC–DC is an informal term used to define someone sexually attracted to both men and women.)

'We split the jobs. The ones who prefer guys, like me, only get men,' he said. When he left GP Gym, Frans moved to DR, which is more open and transparent in its business transactions.

I was already on my third glass of beer when Frans asked me to go to DR. When we got there it was very quiet. There were only two massage boys, three massage girls who were working the night shift and a receptionist. The reception area looked empty.

'Do you want to try to do it with a boy?' Frans teased me when we were in front of the reception desk. I blushed. The receptionist in front of me smiled. That was the first time in my entire life I'd had an offer to sleep with a man, and the offer had been made so openly. I immediately refused. There's no way, I thought to myself through gritted teeth.

'I may not be handsome but I still like women. Do I look like I could be bisexual?' I asked.

'Who knows how deep the ocean is? Who knows if you want to try it this time? Ha ha ...' Frans laughed.

Still speaking in a very matter-of-fact way, he then mentioned the rate at DR, which is the same for massage boys and massage girls. For a one hour 'plus' massage in a standard room the cost is between Rp300,000 (US$36) and Rp400,000 (US$48). This includes the room rent, one soft drink and the full-service treatment.

'The rate is double for outside transactions—between Rp700,000 (US$85) and Rp1 million (US$120). It depends on the negotiation,' he said.

Some time later Frans talked me into booking a massage girl who was working that night. Her name was Linda and he thought she was quite pretty and had a sexy body. He made me curious so finally I said yes. Frans asked her to join us in the reception area. To be honest, Linda wasn't everything she made out to be. She had straight brownish hair, quite big breasts and dark skin. She was wearing a white shirtdress which looked a bit like a nurse's uniform. She smiled and introduced herself.

'Are you sure you don't want to be massaged? You'll regret turning me down once you get home,' she teased. But as I had only gone there to meet Frans, I passed on her offer. Besides, it was getting late and I had got enough information from my chat with Frans.

'Next time, okay? I promise I'll come back here,' I said to Linda. She seemed a little disappointed.

'Promise? I'll wait then,' she said.

I kept my promise. Three days later I went back to DR to test out its sex services. There are ten standard rooms and five VIP rooms. Both types are almost the same, the only difference being that the VIP room is a little bit larger and has a TV.

'If your girlfriends want to have a massage here, tell them to look for me. I guarantee they will become addicted,' said Linda when I later excused myself. I found out that Linda also serves female customers who want to pleasure themselves with their own kind. Oh my god!

The Inside-Out
Teenage Massage Service

There is a massage parlour which offers a special inside-out massage service given by delightful teenage massage girls.

One afternoon in October 2003 I was sipping a cup of hot coffee in one of my favourite cafés in a mall around Senayan while writing this article. A huge storm had just hit Jakarta. Sitting at a nearby table were a group of men and women enjoying their afternoon tea and some snacks. I was surprised because the twelve beautiful ladies at the table were all from Uzbekistan. Most of the café's guests were staring at them in wonder. The reason for all the attention was that they had pretty faces, tall, lean bodies and were wearing sexy outfits which exposed their hot figures. Unfortunately I wasn't really thinking about women at that time. My mind was on a massage parlour in Ancol and the article I was writing. So even though I did glance across at the Uzbekistani girls occasionally, my thoughts were firmly focussed on my laptop.

The massage parlour in Ancol I was writing about had unique services which made it stand out from other massage parlours. The highlight on the menu was an inside-out massage service given by very desirable teenagers.

The Teenage Massage

It was August 2003. That afternoon I was driving towards Ancol for one purpose: to experience for myself the teenage massage service that had become such a hot topic among my clubbing friends. I wasn't alone, of course. My friend Bambang was with me. He is thirty-six years old and works as a contractor on transport projects. In fact, I hardly ever see him. The last time we bumped into him was one Sunday night at HRC in Thamrin. On Sunday nights most clubs are usually closed or pretty dull, but HRC is the opposite. It has become the place to be because the crowd is so hip, even on a Sunday night. At least they have a live music performance which is worth watching.

'Are we going to Ancol just like we planned?' asked Bambang when I met him in quite a crowded café in Plaza Indonesia.

'Sure we are. You're the one who's tried it before; I've only heard about it. You have to be my guide,' I said.

'But you're the one who's paying, right?' he grinned.

'You must be joking, aren't you? You are the one with billion-dollar projects. C'mon, man,' I said.

'You are such a sweet talker, aren't you? Ok, let's go,' Bambang gave in easily.

So at around 5.30 pm that afternoon we both arrived at the teenage parlour called MR. We spotted it easily since it was located among a group of retail shophouses. Other shophouses nearby had been converted into discotheques and MR wasn't very far from these.

The shophouse that housed MR was designed in a very simple way. In the top right corner of the front door was a sign with MR written on it. Cars could park directly in front of the building. There were about eight to ten cars parked there that afternoon. It was getting dark when we arrived. In front of the building there were a group of hawkers selling cigarettes and snacks.

We went inside and sat in the waiting room, which was also a café. Two cups of hot coffee became our companions as the slow afternoon passed. After finishing our coffee we then went to the reception desk and found out that, just like every other massage parlour I have visited, the modus operandi was the same. On the reception desk were pictures of the massage girls. Guests could either browse the pictures or ask the manager or mammi if they could look at the display room. But looking at the display room here wasn't that easy because it was also the waiting room where the girls would hang out waiting for orders. Only members or loyal customers were allowed to go directly to the display room.

'Which one do you want, Mr Bambang?' asked the female receptionist while handing a photo album to Bambang. We browsed the album for about five minutes. On every page there was a picture of a massage girl with a short paragraph about her.

'I've been with this one before.' Bambang pointed to the picture of a girl named Dewi, dressed in a blue shirt. According to Bambang, Dewi was only twenty-one years old and he'd booked her at least once or twice before.

'Is Mr Sofyan in? I'd like to meet him, please,' Bambang requested. He wanted to see the display room.

'Yes, he is. I'll get him for you, just one moment.'

While waiting for Mr Sofyan, who was also called Mr Yan, we went back to the café. Bambang advised me to always see the girl in person rather than rely on a picture.

Mr Sofyan appeared five minutes later. Bambang already knew the guy. To me he looked neat and smart, dressed in a cream shirt and a pair of smart trousers. He joined us at our table and we chatted for a while about the latest news at MR. From that conversation I found out that they had some new 'stock'—new teenage masseuses who'd only been working there a week.

'Let's go to the display room so you gentlemen can take a better look at the girls,' said Mr Yan.

The display room was far from what I'd imagined. Other display rooms I'd seen had a glass wall which separated the girls from the guests. At MR, however, the room was just like a waiting room for the girls. It was on the first floor, at the back, with a flight of stairs leading from the reception desk. In terms of size it wasn't much bigger than a deluxe room in a four-star hotel. When we went in there were twenty girls waiting. Some were sitting comfortably on a sofa, others were watching TV and chatting. A few were lounging on chairs.

Mr Yan allowed us to glance in from the doorway. According to him, the girls were, on average, between twenty-one and thirty-two years old, but there were some who were as young as sixteen. He told us that those under twenty were the most popular.

As soon as the girls realised we were there they started behaving themselves. Some of them smiled and waved to us, others looked a bit shy and surprised. Then I spotted one girl sitting in front of a TV. She looked very young. I chose her to be my date.

'She is called Monik and she's just seventeen years old. So fresh, isn't she?' Mr Yan prompted with a little laugh. Bambang chose to reunite with Dewi, his long-term, twenty-three-year-old partner.

'I don't like to take chances with this. I've been with Dewi twice, the last time being two months ago. She was great,' said Bambang.

We'd been at the display room less than fifteen minutes when Mr Yan asked us to book a VIP room. The rooms were also on the first floor and only ten metres from the display room. Monik and Dewi got ready to perform. Background music filled every single room in the parlour.

Bambang and I took VIP rooms next to each other. My VIP room was no different to a standard room in a three-star hotel. It had air-con, a chair, a table, a shower and a bed which was covered with white sheets. Music filled the room and the lighting was quite dim. Monik appeared ten minutes later. She'd put on some make-up and looked fresher than before. She had blusher on her cheeks and her lips were painted peach. It went well with her fair skin and her outfit. Her long hair hung around her shoulders.

'Hi, have you been waiting long?' she greeted me.

I took a closer look at her appearance. She was not more than 165 cm tall and the pink shirtdress and high heels she was wearing made her look older. It would be easy to mistake her for at least twenty years old, rather than seventeen. I tried to make conversation and break the ice. Even though the transaction was one of buy and sell, I felt uncomfortable dating someone I barely knew. Usually I knew at least the basics, like name, age, origin and how long they had worked in that place.

After I thought we'd been introduced enough, we moved onto the massage service. Even though it was only her third week at MR, Monik seemed quite comfortable and confident. She was polite and friendly, even when she suggested that we begin the transaction.

'So, do you want to start now or would you prefer to just chat?' she joked. Quite frankly, that kind of talk turns me on.

'If we continue talking, the time will fly. Don't you feel bad ignoring such a beautiful girl like me?' she teased, cooling down the temperature of the room.

'Ok, let's get it on then,' I said, half joking.

'Are you sure? Don't you want me to give you an introduction first? Let's start slowly, but I guarantee you'll enjoy it very much,' she giggled.

Of course, what she meant by introduction was foreplay. In some massage parlours foreplay comes in different varieties, ranging from a sexy massage on erotic zones to oral sex. At MR, foreplay consists of a sexy massage or the cat bath service.

A short-time date in a VIP room at MR usually lasts for an hour. If guests want longer, they have to pay for two hours. This usually happens when guests aren't satisfied with one hour. The rate for one hour is Rp300,000 (US$36), not including tips.

'Are you sure you don't want longer? Do you really want to go home now? You'll regret it later,' Monik teased.

The Other Side of Monik

MR parlour has twelve teenage masseuses the same age as Monik. Some of them are freelancers while others work full-time. It was only after going to MR three or four times that I was able to talk to Monik as a friend. She told me her side of the story, and why she was living like this at her age. She was from Sukabumi, Jawa Barat and in the beginning she'd been a typical teenager living in a small village. One day two 'talent scouts' came to the village. Usually talent scouts work for advertising agencies or production houses, but these days a lot of nightclubs also employ them. The two who came to Monik's village had been told about her by her friends in the same village. They also worked at MR.

Monik had only just graduated from junior high school and was helping her parents, who were just peasants. So when these two guys came and offered Monik Rp10 million (US$1,200) to take her to Jakarta and work as a massage girl, her parents didn't hesitate at all. Money was their main motivation. Who wouldn't say yes to Rp10 million (US$1,200) when you have to work hard on a farm and your income depends on that season's harvest?

'I said yes because they offered me a big salary. Besides, my parents had already said yes,' said Monik, who had met me in a café in Gunung Sahari. It was her day off. She told me she has one day off a week and each girl can choose the day, as long as it's not Friday, Saturday or Sunday.

'I take Monday off because usually it's not busy,' she said while sipping a glass of cold orange juice.

She told me that when they brought her to Jakarta they didn't tell her where she was going to work. All she knew was that she was going to work in some cosmetic company and get paid Rp2 million (US$240) per month. Such a tempting offer made her very eager to go to Jakarta. She thought that with such a good salary she could ease her parent's financial worries. She is the eldest of three. When she left, her brother and sister were very young. One was still in the fourth grade and the other was just two years old.

When she arrived in Jakarta, Monik didn't work immediately. She was placed in a big house around Mangga Besar and had her training there. She wasn't alone. At least fourteen other girls were with her and two mammies coordinated their daily schedules.

The training, which lasted for two weeks, was more like personality training. The girls were taught how to speak, to pose and to groom themselves. Monik said she was shocked when she found out that her job was to be a 'plus' masseuse, something that had never even crossed her mind. She first found out from a rumour between the other girls. Then, when the training was about to end, the mammi announced it officially. She didn't really know how to react.

'There was no way I could say no. I couldn't run away because I didn't know anything about Jakarta,' she explained.

One time she will never forget is the first night she had to serve a customer in a hotel room. The mammi took advantage of her virginity and 'sold' it to a man for a lot of money. She couldn't escape from the reality that she was being sold and had to obey her master. So she was forced to give her virginity to a complete stranger in a four-star hotel room. For the first time in her entire life too, she had money—but she still doesn't know for sure how much the mammi sold her virginity for.

'I never had that much money before, you know. Not even Rp100,000 (US$12),' said Monik. The first time she didn't ask for anything extra. She just knew that she had to do her job right. Even though her experiences have been bitterly painful, Monik told me her story without showing any emotion.

After that first night she spent the next two months as a call girl, serving guests from one hotel to another. For every transaction she did she was paid Rp1 million (US$120) in cold hard cash. By contrast the mammi charged Rp3 million (US$360) to Rp5 million (US$600). Monik could command such high prices because the mammi would brag that Monik was just a teenager and new to the sex industry.

After two months Monik was sent to the massage parlour at MR as a full-time masseuse. Despite being full-time, however, she does have private outside orders. At MR, for every Rp300,000 (US$36) short-time transaction, she gets a share of Rp125,000 (US$15). Tips go directly into her pocket. The mammi or management have no right to interfere with the tips.

'Sometimes if I serve a guest well I get a much higher tip,' said Monik, who looked more mature than most girls her age.

When I met her, Monik had been a sex worker for almost two years, helping her family pay the bills with the money she earnt through sex. They renovated their house in the village, bought new paddy fields and were able to buy daily groceries. She told me that she had no idea how long she would work as a massage girl. Experience had taught her so much, especially about how hard life can be. In her seventeen years she was definitely more mature because of what she had seen in the sex industry.

'I hope I can open my own business when I have enough money. It's really tiring working like this. Besides, I am still young, I have plenty of opportunities ahead,' she said.

I almost forgot to mention that Monik is only an alias. Her real name is Nana Juliana since she was born sometime in July. She told me she often forgets her real name since the name Monik has been glued to her head for the past two years. She said that if the time ever comes for her to get out of her present job, she wants very much to go back to being the old Juliana, a naïve village girl. The question is, when?

'I don't know yet. For now I just do what I have to do. It's just so tiring thinking about it too seriously,' she said.

Night had fallen. After finishing a plate of calamari, Monik excused herself and left. She is just one of thousands and thousands of teenagers who, accidentally or not, have been caught up in the sex industry. In hundreds of nightclubs across Jakarta many many Moniks face the same fate.

Cocktail Girls
in V-VIP Rooms

In some top hotels, pretty girls are served as appetisers and desserts. They are famously known as 'cocktail girls'.

Three girls sat gracefully on a black sofa. One was wearing a sexy gown, one a micro miniskirt. The first girl let her long hair hang down and touch her open back. She was wearing a pair of high heels and a blue gown that glowed under the yellowish lights. The second girl had short hair, delicate fair skin and her face was a bit round. She was wearing a micro miniskirt with a tight top and a brown jacket. The third girl wore a black cocktail dress. Her make-up made her face look radiantly beautiful. Her white teeth shone when she smiled and her lips were beautifully painted with red lipstick.

At the same time three guys were sitting on another black sofa nearby. They couldn't help but stare and smile at the girls. Once the ice had been broken, both parties started to get more familiar with each other. They were laughing and chatting flirtatiously.

The room was painted in bold colours. Red, black and orange blended beautifully as if the room itself was a big canvas. There were long sofas, some glass chairs and two twenty-one-inch TVs, which were the focus of the room.

'I'm Cindy. I'm twenty-two years old and come from Bandung.'

'I am Lenny. I am only nineteen years old, and am still single. I come from Sukabumi and I've worked here for six months.'

'I am Vivi. I am twenty-three years old and I am from Malang. I used to be a model but then I quit to try out new things.'

Cindy, Lenny and Vivi were the names of the three girls who were serving their three clients. But, of course, Cindy, Lenny and Vivi aren't their real names. It is common knowledge that almost every girl who works at a karaoke bar, a massage parlour, a love house, a nightclub or a sauna never uses her real name. Take Cindy from Bandung, for instance. Her real name is Maemuna, Lenny is Kustini and Vivi confessed that her real name is Juwariah.

It has become a trend among the girls who work in nightclubs to have an alias that is catchy, modern and easy to remember. Sometimes management give the alias to the girl. That's why so many LCs, strippers, karaoke singers, massage girls and call girls always have such cool and hip names. Cindy, Lenny and Vivi are just three names among thousands which light up Jakarta's nightlife.

V-VIP Hotel

That night the girls, who were actually LCs, continued showing their clients great hospitality. They were in Flamboyant Hotel's karaoke club which is located in Jalan JSP, Jakarta Barat. The brightly designed, four-star hotel is along a main road and stands out from all the other buildings nearby. For more than a year it has been considered a hip place for guys who want to relax in luxurious rooms or just have fun at the karaoke bar or at the massage parlour in the company of beautiful girls.

Cindy, Lenny and Vivi are only three of the beautiful cocktail girls who set the atmosphere in the karaoke bar or the hotel rooms. Their job is the same as LCs in other karaoke clubs: to keep guests company while they relax, sing or drink. Sometimes the girls offer extra services, such as sex, depending on the agreement.

At first I doubted whether the cocktail girls in the Flamboyant Hotel were really giving extra services, services which are supposedly available day and night. What I have heard is that the Flamboyant Hotel is famous for its V-VIP (double VIP) sex services. The hotel is known to have full facilities with a karaoke bar, a massage parlour, a salon and a sauna. Guests can check into several different types of rooms.

Out of curiosity, I went there with my friend Dimas. He is a thirty-one-year-old bachelor who works for a Japanese car company in Pondok Indah. Even though he is over thirty, he's definitely not ready to tie the knot. He told me he is afraid of having a family and all the responsibility, rules and demands which go with it. That's why every time I ask him when he's getting married, he just grins.

'I am not ready yet. Besides, I haven't finished enjoying my youth. I still want to be free,' he said, then giggled.

At around 9 pm Dimas and I were already in the car park of the Flamboyant Hotel. We parked at B2. From there we went to the lobby. Of course we didn't want to check in, just have a look around. As usual, the lobby was a bit busy with people milling around the reception desk. Some people were sitting on a sofa and to the right of the reception desk there was a lounge where a few couples were occupying tables under the dim lighting, listening to romantic music. The lobby was also brightly lit up. Glass panels covered sections of the walls and reflected the white ceiling lights. We didn't stay long in the lobby, and after five minutes took the lift to the first floor where the karaoke bar was. At the entrance there was a reception desk manned by two female receptionists. They greeted us in a friendly manner and offered us a selection of interesting packages. There were three suite rooms, two VIP rooms and three standard rooms available.

'Can we have a VIP room? We don't need to wait, do we?' asked Dimas.

'No, you don't. There are two rooms left. But why don't you gentlemen order the suite room? It has another room attached,' said the receptionist.

'No thanks. It's just the two of us so why do we need an attached room?' Dimas asked, pretending to be naïve.

'You're just pretending you don't know, right, boss? Your room is 104,' said the receptionist jokingly. A waiter showed us to our room. We waited on a white sofa for a few moments before the LCs' coordinator came over to us. She gave us a few names of the girls available that evening. Among the names she mentioned were Vivi and Cindy. Our friends, who had been to Flamboyant Hotel many times, told us to take a look at the display room or ask the mammi to bring the girls into the room. Finally we chose Cindy and Vivi.

'You take Cindy and I'll take Vivi, okay, Jo?' Dimas called me Jo as it is an informal greeting in Indonesia, similar to Bro, Brur or Man.

'Okay, no problem.'

While we were waiting for Cindy and Vivi we ordered snacks, fruit platters and two bottles of Corona beer. We also ordered my favourite drink, a Black Russian, and Dimas' favourite drink, a Flaming Bikini. A Flaming Bikini is a liquor which is served while still burning, then drunk in a single shot.

Not long after that, Cindy and Vivi appeared. Both these sexy beautiful girls were everything our friends had told us they were. Cindy is quite slim and has long hair, while Vivi is of average height and has a plump figure. Some of our friends think that Vivi has a voluptuous killer body. The tight outfit she was wearing made her figure seem even more gorgeous. She looked sophisticated and no one would have guessed she was from a quiet small town called Teretes, Jawa Timur.

When the girls arrived they ordered their favourite drinks. They introduced themselves and we all got along very well. As professional LCs they adapted very easily to the situation and both seemed very easy going. Even though they'd just met us, they made us feel as if we were old friends. Before the girls arrived, the room had been filled with loud music from the TV. That was now replaced with laughter and flirtatious giggles. Both girls were also quite good singers and could sing both pop and Dangdut very well.

For three hours we had a great time with Cindy and Vivi, just like couples who were madly in love. We enjoyed every moment we spent together on the comfortable sofa, the cool breeze from the air-con engulfing the whole room. Alcohol was free flowing, and Cindy and Vivi teased us with their coquettish behaviour which, of course, was very seductive. They pinched us tender-heartedly, hugged us, rested their heads on our shoulders and so on.

The scent of Bvlgari Extreme perfume which emanated from Vivi's body was intoxicating. Cindy's scent by Issey Miyake was equally seductive and sexy. After a while we were all so intimate that we started performing small sex acts. Of course, we knew that if we offered them a sex date they would probably say yes, as long as we'd already agreed the fee in advance.

'Don't you want more? Are you sure you just want to be hugged?' teased Vivi.

'Yes, c'mon boys ... seriously, don't you want something hotter than this?' Cindy rested her head seductively on Dimas' shoulder.

The VIP room we'd rented didn't have a bedroom, unlike the suite. Usually the bedroom is where the sex takes place. Some of the cocktail girls in Flamboyant Hotel also give sex as part of the service.

Cindy, who had so much energy, was trying to plant the idea of sex into Dimas' head. She tried to tempt him several times into having sex because if they only get the tip, they can end up with around Rp200,000 (US$24) to Rp300,000 (US$36) for the whole three hours. If they are very lucky and get a generous guest, they can get a big tip without having to have sex.

'But a big tipper like that only happens once in a blue moon. Not many guests give Rp500,000 (US$60) as a tip for just getting hugged,' said Vivi. That was why a sex date is the final service a cocktail girl can offer to ensure she gets at least Rp1 million (US$120) for one short time.

Being a normal guy, Dimas finally gave in to Cindy's nonstop hot temptation. Since there was no bedroom in the VIP room, they both excused themselves to the attached bathroom where they agreed to seal the deal. In some karaoke rooms that don't have bedrooms it is quite common to finish the sex date in the bathroom. Sometimes it is just a hand job, oral sex or, of course, full service. For some guys, having sex in a bathroom is quite sensational and boosts their sense of adventure. It makes a change from doing it in the bedroom.

'Sorry, we go inside first. I can't wait much longer,' said Dimas, his face red from alcohol.

Vivi and I were still sitting on the sofa. Seeing Cindy conquor Dimas gave Vivi the incentive to try even harder to seduce me. She started acting even bolder than before. The micro miniskirt that she was wearing made her bare legs look even more beautiful. I felt like I was watching a bikini contest. So eventually what was happening in the bathroom was also happening on the sofa. The night was getting hotter, not only from the influence of alcohol but also from the passionate sex acts that even the room's air-con system couldn't cool down.

Our three hours ran out just after the sex date had finished. We went home, driving along the Thamrin road.

'You said we were just going to have a chat, but it turned out to be pretty wild, man,' I teased Dimas.

'C'mon, I'm a normal guy. There was no way I could resist her advances. I lost Rp1 million (US$120) from taking the bathroom service,' said Dimas.

'You have to be patient. I only gave her Rp500,000 (US$60) as a tip and I also got the extra service.'

'I don't care. As long as I am happy,' Dimas said.

'We should've rented the suite, but we didn't really know at the time.'

'Yes, but it's boring to do it on the bed all the time. It's more challenging in the bathroom, ha ha.' Dimas laughed loudly. His blew out the smoke from his Dji Sam Soe cigarette. We stopped for a while at Sabang street to eat fried rice with omelette and corned beef.

The Cocktail Girls

A cocktail girl is actually no different to a female escort or LC. The only difference is that cocktail girls are more likely to give sexual services than LCs. Cocktail girl is just a euphemism for hostess, call girl, female escort or commercial sex worker. The term takes its name from cocktails, which are also popular and associated with a good time. And just like the drinks come with different names, so too do the girls: female escort, singer, madam and nightclub girl.

In Surabaya, for instance, the latest popular name for a cocktail girl is *purel*. Such names identify the girls who work in the nightclubs, karaoke bars and private homes. Their main job is to keep guests company, making them as comfortable as they can so that they don't hesitate to spend as much money as possible—even offer a sex date if necessary. These names identify the girls in the illicit world in which they work.

At the Flamboyant Hotel the cocktail girls are divided into several groups. The first group contains those who work full-time, the second group consists of those who work as freelancers and the third group is those who work as exotic dancers or strippers. But almost all of them are willing to give sex services. Of course, the date doesn't always end up in bed, but most are willing to perform some kind of small sex act such as oral sex or something else. The official charge for a cocktail girl is Rp45,000 (US$5.50) per hour for a minimum of seven hours. That means a total cost of around Rp315,000 (US$38). But for that price the guests only get a companion to sing and drink with, nothing more. If the guest wants extra services he has to spend at least another Rp500,000 (US$60) or more.

Another thing about these cocktail girls is the fact that not all of them want to have a sex date on the premises. Some of them prefer to do it outside the nightclub. The rate depends on the negotiation. Since it is an outside service, the date takes place outside of booking hours, but if the sex date takes place at the Flamboyant Hotel, it is a different story. Booking a sex date at the hotel is an option for guests who don't want to waste time or money in the karaoke room.

'Many guests want to book at sex date at in a hotel room. The rate is Rp1.5 million (US$180) cash, no credit cards allowed,' said Cindy.

The transaction process is very simple. The guest appears in the karaoke club to meet the coordinator of the cocktail girls and place his order. He can choose a girl from the display room, from pictures or from one recommended by the coordinator.

'It saves a lot of money that way because you don't have to pay for F&B, the rental fee for the karaoke room or tips,' said Dimas, who had checked into the Flamboyant Hotel three or four times already.

An exotic dancer or stripper who is also a cocktail girl in the Flamboyant Hotel has the same duty. She gives exotic performances and usually says yes to the offer of a sex date. These girls are similar to strippers in elite nightclubs, who also expect big tips from giving sex services after the show. If the girls only depend on the rate of the show, they only earn Rp450,000 (US$55). That's why they need to 'give' more to get more money.

Flamboyant Hotel's karaoke club is famous among high society. Top executives, high commissioners, businessmen and even male celebrities are often seen there. Cindy and Vivi, who have been in the business for almost a year, told me that they have served a few male celebrities. They mentioned actors like RP, YD and WP who went to the karaoke bar with small groups of friends to sing and be accompanied by beautiful cocktail girls or see a striptease show.

'After karaoke, some of them book a room straightaway,' said Vivi.

When Vivi and Cindy knew they'd been booked by famous actors, they didn't really care about the tips. For them there was a certain pride in having dated a famous guy. They never even bothered to negotiate, and gave the actors everything they wanted.

'If we have big tips, we are lucky, but small tips are okay too. It's not like every day we have a celebrity as our date,' said Cindy. She told me that once she was booked to accompany a guy to dinner in a restaurant and he paid Rp300,000 (US$36) to Rp500,000 (US$60) for the service. For that kind of transaction the coordinator plays a big part.

The presence of cocktail girls is getting more and more popular in some hotels which also provided 'extra' entertainment. Flamboyant Hotel isn't the only one. There is LM Hotel around Blok M, Jakarta Selatan which also highlights cocktail girls on its menu and has a standard rate of Rp300,000 (US$36) per night. They have even reserved the eighth floor just for this purpose. There, guests can receive the tender touch of cocktail girls and check in to the hotel for as little as one hour.

The Flamboyant Hotel has a karaoke bar and massage parlour, whereas the LM Hotel only uses a massage parlour. Another difference is that the Flamboyant Hotel also provides imported cocktail girls from China, the Philippines and Thailand, whilst at LM Hotel you can only find local cocktail girls. That is why the rate is different. One date with a cocktail girl in the Flamboyant costs between Rp1 million (US$120) and Rp3 million (US$360), while in LM Hotel it is only Rp350,000 (US$40) per short time.

'The facilities a place has is a significant factor when it comes to pricing, even though the end result is still the same,' said Dimas, who was starting to get sleepy after being fully satisfied, both mentally and physically, if you know what I mean.

SOURCES

1. 'The Midnight Lesbian Package' was published in *Male Emporium*, under the title 'Special Midnite Hotel Package', Nitelife column, 25 February 2003.

2. 'The Love House Of The Kawanua Girls' was published in *Male Emporium* under the title 'The Kawanua Girls in Rose Apartment', Nitelife column, 22 September 2002.

3. 'A One-Night Stand With The Mickey Mouse Girls' was published in *Male Emporium*, Nitelife column, October 2002.

4. 'The Take-Half-Your-Clothes-Off Party' was published in *Djakarta*, the city and life magazine, under the title of 'Dressing Across Party, Topless Party & Gigolo Party', May 2003.

5. Terence T. Hull, Endang Sulistyaningsih & Gavin W. Jones, *Prostitution in Indonesia: History and Development,* published by Pustaka Sinar Harapan in corporation with Ford Foundation, referred to in the article 'The Monkey Business of Libido Sprees'.

6. *Popular Magazine*, December 1997 edition, special feature column, 'Calculating the Sex Business' Revenue' for the article 'The Monkey Business of Libido Sprees'.

7. Thanh-Dam Truong, *Sex, Money, and Morality: Prostitution and Tourism in Southeast Asia,* published by LP3S, first edition, June 1992, for the article 'The Monkey Business of Libido Sprees'.

8. GAYa Bulletin Nusantara, Surabaya, September 2002 edition for the article 'Gay Night and Lesbian Society'.

9. A bulletin for *GAYa Nusantara*, Surabaya, January 2003 edition for 'Gay Night and Lesbian Society' article.

10. http://swara.cjb.net or http://welcom.to/swara-srikandi for the article 'Gay Nite and Lesbian Society'.

11. http://welcome.to/gaya

12. http://babyjimaditya.com